High School Reunion: The Musical

Book and Lyrics by
Billy Van Zandt
and **Jane Milmore**

Music by **Billy Van Zandt,
Jane Milmore,**
and **Nick DeGregorio**

A SAMUEL FRENCH ACTING EDITION

NEW YORK HOLLYWOOD LONDON TORONTO

SAMUELFRENCH.COM

Book and Lyrics Copyright © 2011 by Billy Van Zandt Living Trust
and Jane Milmore Living Trust

ALL RIGHTS RESERVED

Cover Photography by Danny Sanchez
Cover Graphic Design by Noel Kubel
Actors Pictured: Glenn Jones, Sally Winters, Billy Van Zandt, Jane Milmore, Ed Carlo, Susan Travers, and (on floor) Barbara Bonilla

CAUTION: Professionals and amateurs are hereby warned that *HIGH SCHOOL REUNION: THE MUSICAL* is subject to a licensing fee. It is fully protected under the copyright laws of the United States of America, the British Commonwealth, including Canada, and all other countries of the Copyright Union. All rights, including professional, amateur, motion picture, recitation, lecturing, public reading, radio broadcasting, television and the rights of translation into foreign languages are strictly reserved. In its present form the play is dedicated to the reading public only.

The amateur and professional live stage performance rights to *HIGH SCHOOL REUNION: THE MUSICAL* are controlled exclusively by Samuel French, Inc., and licensing arrangements and performance licenses must be secured well in advance of presentation. PLEASE NOTE that amateur licensing fees are set upon application in accordance with your producing circumstances. When applying for a licensing quotation and a performance license please give us the number of performances intended, dates of production, your seating capacity and admission fee. Licensing fees are payable one week before the opening performance of the play to Samuel French, Inc., at 45 W. 25th Street, New York, NY 10010.

Licensing fee of the required amount must be paid whether the play is presented for charity or gain and whether or not admission is charged.

Professional/Stock licensing fees quoted upon application to Samuel French, Inc.

For all other rights than those stipulated above, apply to: Samuel French, Inc., 45 West 25th Street, New York, NY 10010.

Particular emphasis is laid on the question of amateur or professional readings, permission and terms for which must be secured in writing from Samuel French, Inc.

Copying from this book in whole or in part is strictly forbidden by law, and the right of performance is not transferable.

Whenever the play is produced the following notice must appear on all programs, printing and advertising for the play: "Produced by special arrangement with Samuel French, Inc."

Due authorship credit must be given on all programs, printing and advertising for the play.

ISBN 978-0-573-69962-7   Printed in U.S.A.   #29935

No one shall commit or authorize any act or omission by which the copyright of, or the right to copyright, this play may be impaired.

No one shall make any changes in this play for the purpose of production.

Publication of this play does not imply availability for performance. Both amateurs and professionals considering a production are strongly advised in their own interests to apply to Samuel French, Inc., for written permission before starting rehearsals, advertising, or booking a theatre.

No part of this book may be reproduced, stored in a retrieval system, or transmitted in any form, by any means, now known or yet to be invented, including mechanical, electronic, photocopying, recording, videotaping, or otherwise, without the prior written permission of the publisher.

RENTAL MATERIALS

An orchestration consisting of **Bass, Drums, Guitar, Reed, Synth, Piano Vocal Score and a Full Conductor Score** will be loaned two months prior to the production ONLY on the receipt of the Licensing Fee quoted for all performances, the rental fee and a refundable deposit.

Please contact Samuel French for perusal of the music materials as well as a performance license application.

IMPORTANT BILLING AND CREDIT REQUIREMENTS

All producers of *HIGH SCHOOL REUNION: THE MUSICAL* must give credit to the Author of the Play in all programs distributed in connection with performances of the Play, and in all instances in which the title of the Play appears for the purposes of advertising, publicizing or otherwise exploiting the Play and/or a production. The name of the Author *must* appear on a separate line on which no other name appears, immediately following the title and *must* appear in size of type not less than fifty percent of the size of the title type.

In addition the following credit *must* be given in all programs and publicity information distributed in association with this piece:

Book & Lyrics By
Billy Van Zandt and Jane Milmore

Original Music by
Billy Van Zandt, Jane Milmore and Nick DeGregorio

Arrangements & Orchestrations by
Nick DeGregorio

HIGH SCHOOL REUNION: THE MUSICAL opened Friday, May 15, 2009 at the Brookdale College Performing Arts Center, Lincroft, New Jersey, under the direction of Gary Shaffer. It was produced by Jack Ryan and Noel Kubel. Musical direction, orchestrations, and arrangements were by Nick DeGregorio. Choreographer was Michele Mossay. Conductor was Colin Freeman. Costume design was by Kitty Cleary. Light and Sound design were by Chris Woolley. Property Mistress was Jen Lucero. Stage Manager was Lauren Cervasio. Graphic design was by Kevin Cosme. Photography by Danny Sanchez. The cast, in order of appearance, was as follows:

DEBBIE POLICASTRO	Susan Travers
AMY AARON	Lynn Kroll
FRED "THE HEAD" COLICCHIO	Bob Thompson
TUG FENDERMACHER	Charles F. Wagner IV
CALVIN GIBLIN	Jeff Babey
BUTCH FUORRY	Michael Chartier
JOHNNY OCHES	Art Neill
SIMON GROUPIE	Glenn Jones
MIKE TERZANO	Michael Kroll
BARBARA JEAN BEHLENDORF	Sally Winters
BOB FIELDS	Tom Frascatore
MARSHA FIELDS	Jackie Neill
TOMMY BEEKMAN	Billy Van Zandt
CHRISTIE O'CONNOR	Barbara Bonilla
JULIE RYAN	Jane Milmore
MISS BLUMQUIST	Kathy Reed
MR. STINITSKI	Brian Fuorry
TODD FINLEY	Ed Carlo

CHARACTERS

TOMMY BEEKMAN – "most likely to succeed"
CHRISTIE – the homecoming queen
JULIE RYAN – the prettiest girl
DEBBIE POLICASTRO – the head cheerleader
TODD FINLEY – the closeted gay kid
SENATOR BOB FIELDS – the class president
MARSHA FIELDS – the perfect politician's wife
TUG FENDERMACHER – the football hero
BARBARA JEAN BEHLENDORF – the class slut
CALVIN GIBLIN – the class clown
FRED "THE HEAD" COLICCHIO – the class stoner
AMY AARON – the class valedictorian
JOHNNY OCHES – the kid with the guitar
SIMON GROUPIE – the kid no one noticed
BUTCH FUORRY – the kid who smells
MIKE TERZANO – the party crasher
MISS BLUMQUIST – the hot teacher

MUSICAL NUMBERS

ACT ONE

I Hope They Know Me	COMPANY
Back In High School	DEBBIE
Fugue for Alumni	CALVIN, BUTCH FUORRY, TUG, JOHNNY
Is It You	BARBARA JEAN
I Am	BOB AND COMPANY
Faking It	TOMMY, CHRISTINE
Conceited Bitch Polka	COMPANY
Miss Blunquist	CALVIN
Julie	MEN
Back in High School (Reprise)	DEBBIE
Garden State of Mind	JULIE
Don't Drop The Ball	TUG, COMPANY
Boy Scouts USA	VILLAGE PERSON
Fabulous	TODD, COMPANY

ACT TWO

Mike Terzano	MIKE TERZANO
Christina	COMPANY
Blumquist's Turn	MISS BLUMQUIST
I'll Never Dance With You	DEBBIE, TODD
You Are Mine	TOMMY, CHRISTINE
I Have Waited a Lifetime	TUG, JULIE
It Is You	BARBARA JEAN, BOB, MARSHA, TODD
I'll Be There	JOHNNY, COMPANY
Boomers	COMPANY

ACT 1

Scene One

*(**SETTING**: Empty hall)*

*(**AT RISE**: OVERTURE begins. The stage goes to black. Lights up: Limbo. Fourteen people holding their class photos in front of their faces. They drop the photos down and sing [a la "Chorus Line"].)*

*(**Song**: "I HOPE THEY KNOW ME")*

ALL.
> GOD, I HOPE THEY KNOW ME
> I HOPE THEY KNOW ME

WOMEN.
> I'VE CHANGED SO MUCH SINCE WAY BACK THEN

MEN.
> I'VE CHANGED SO MUCH SINCE WAY BACK THEN

WOMEN.
> I HOPE THEY KNOW ME

MEN.
> I HOPE THEY KNOW ME

AMY.
> I CANNOT WEAR THE THINGS I WORE

JOHNNY.
> THERE IS NO HAIR HERE ANYMORE

BARBARA JEAN.
> I DON'T REMEMBER HOW TO DANCE

TOMMY.
> OH, JESUS, I CAN'T CLOSE MY PANTS

WOMEN.
>THEY ALL BE STARING
>AT WHAT I'M WEARING
>I'VE CHANGED SO MUCH SINCE WAY BACK THEN

MEN.
>I'VE CHANGED SO MUCH SINCE WAY BACK THEN

WOMEN.
>I'M NOT THAT CUTE GIRL ANYMORE

MEN.
>I'M NOT THAT CUTE BOY ANYMORE

WOMEN.
>I'M NOT THAT CUTE GIRL

ALL.
>ANYMORE
>I'M NOT THAT CUTE –

CHRISTIE.
>OH, GOD…DON'T LET THEM LAUGH
>IN SCHOOL MY SIZE WAS HALF
>DEAR GOD, PLEASE, DON'T LET THEM LAUGH….

(Dance break with drum accents, as people button clothes, check themselves out in mirrors and squeeze into pants.)

CHRISTIE.
>I'VE GOTTEN FAT

MEN.
>I'VE GOTTEN OLD

ALL.
>I'VE GOTTEN GREY
>MY CHIN HAS FOLDS
>GOD, I HOPE THEY KNOW ME
>I HOPE THEY KNOW ME

WOMEN.
>I'VE CHANGED SO MUCH SINCE WAY BACK THEN

MEN.
>I'VE CHANGED SO MUCH SINCE WAY BACK THEN

WOMEN.
>I'LL SUCK IT IN

MEN.
>I'LL STAND UP STRAIGHT

WOMEN.
>I'LL DYE MY HAIR

ALL.
>I'LL LOSE SOME WEIGHT

WOMEN.
>I'LL LEAVE MY GLASSES HERE AT HOME

MEN.
>I'LL DO THE FAKE COMB-OVER COMB

WOMEN.
>DON'T LET THEM MOCK
>DON'T LET THEM POINT

FRED "THE HEAD".
>I'M GONNA SMOKE AN EXTRA JOINT

WOMEN.
>DON'T LET THEM LAUGH

MEN.
>DON'T LET ME CURSE

WOMEN.
>I'LL HIDE MY STOMACH WITH MY PURSE

ALL.
>PLEASE GOD, LET THEM…LOOK WORSE….!
>
>*(blackout)*

Scene Two

(SETTING: School hallway – reception area)

(AT RISE: **DEBBIE** POLICASTRO, *the organizer, is setting up her sign-in table.* **DEBBIE** *wears a name tag that reads "HI, MY NAME IS DEBBIE POLICASTRO" – with a heart over the "i".)*

(Song: "BACK IN HIGH SCHOOL")

DEBBIE.
>HERE IS MY LOCKER
>IT SMELLS THE SAME
>DOWN THERE'S MY HOME ROOM
>BOTH TODD AND I WERE IN IT
>I'M RELIVING EVERY MINUTE
>BACK IN HIGH SCHOOL
>BACK IN HIGH SCHOOL
>PEP RALLY FRIDAYS
>AND S.A.T.S
>WE'D ALL GET HICKEYS
>DOWN UNDERNEATH THE BLEACHERS
>THEN WE'D HIDE THEM FROM THE TEACHERS
>BACK IN HIGH SCHOOL
>BACK IN HIGH SCHOOL
>SIMPLE TIME
>CLASS BELL'S CHIME
>TOLD US WHEN TO MOVE ON
>FREE FROM CARE
>LONG STRAIGHT HAIR
>WHERE HAS TIME GONE?
>WE WERE SO CLOSE THEN
>NOW NO ONE CALLS
>THERE'S JUST THE ECHO
>OF DREAMS WE LEFT BEHIND US
>LET'S GO BACK SO THEY CAN FIND US
>LET'S GO BACK
>BACK TO HIGH SCHOOL

*(A musical interlude where we see **DEBBIE** and **TODD** from the past.)*

DEBBIE. *(cont.)*
WE HAD DREAMS
WE HAD SCHEMES
WE HAD EVERYTHING THEN
WHERE'D IT GO?
I DON'T KNOW
I'M HOME AGAIN!
I FEEL SO SAFE HERE
I COULD JUST CRY
I LOVE THIS HIGH SCHOOL
I LOVE EVERYTHING ABOUT IT
I'VE COME HOME AND I WILL SHOUT IT!
GLAD I'M BACK
BACK IN HIGH SCHOOL!
OUT ON THE QUAD
GAZING AT TODD
THIS NIGHT COULD BE MY LAST CHANCE
FOR TODD AND OUR TRUE ROMANCE
I AM BACK IN HIGH SCHOOL!

*(Eight classmates enter, abuzz with catching up. **AMY AARON**, soccer mom; **FRED "THE HEAD"**, the class stoner; **CALVIN**, the class clown; **JOHNNY**, the musician, complete with his guitar case; **BUTCH**, the former kid-who-smells; **MIKE TERZANO**, ladies man; **TUG**, the ex-jock; and **SIMON**, the guy nobody remembers.)*

AMY. Debbie Policastro!

DEBBIE. Amy Aaron! Omigod, you look exactly the same. Exactly.

AMY. I've been dieting for two months. I was determined I was going to fit into this dress.

DEBBIE. Well, you did it. Sign in over there.

*(**AMY** turns to sign in and we see the seam on the back of her dress is split open.)*

FRED "THE HEAD". Hey, Deb. Frederick Colicchio.

DEBBIE. Fred "the Head." I can't believe it's been thirty years. What have you been doing – thirty years?

FRED "THE HEAD". I'm glad my battles with law enforcement are still a source of amusement to you. I'll have you know…what was the question?

CALVIN. *(to* **JOHNNY***)* You brought your guitar?

JOHNNY. You never know. People are always asking me to play.

BUTCH. What people?

SIMON. Hi, Debbie.

DEBBIE. Are you with the caterer? You're supposed to enter through the cafeteria. Tug!! Our star running back!

(**DEBBIE** *and* **TUG** *hug.*)

TUG. Remember this?

(**TUG** *poses in a Heisman trophy stance.*)

DEBBIE. Everybody remembers that!

SIMON. I'm not a caterer. I'm Simon. Simon Groupie. I sat in front of you in biology. I lived next door to you.

(**DEBBIE** *and* **TUG** *stare at* **SIMON** *– no idea who he is.*
MIKE TERZANO *reads the name on Debbie's name tag.*)

MIKE TERZANO. Debbie Policastro! It's Mike Terzano! My one regret in high school was that I never got to date you. But I never stood a chance against…what was his name?

DEBBIE. Todd. I hear he's divorced now.

(looking at sign-in table)

Oh, my. Mike. I don't think I have a name tag for you. I'm so embarrassed.

(**DEBBIE** *makes one with magic marker.*)

CALVIN. I see London. I see France. I see you buy your underwear at Costco.

(Everyone laughs.)

AMY. You're still the class clown, Calvin.

CALVIN. I know you are, but what am I?

(Song: "FUGUE FOR ALUMNI)

I LIKE TO JOKE AND SHOCK
HERE'S ONE YOU'LL KNOW – KNOCK KNOCK
I'LL PUT NAIR HAIR REMOVER INSIDE YOUR JOCK
LOOK THERE
NO HAIR
YOUR BAD STUTTER I WILL M-M-MOCK
DOWN MY PANTS I WILL STUFF A SOCK
WHAT'S THIS?

(pulls out a rubber chicken)

MY CHICKEN!

BUTCH FUORRY.

I WAS THE BOY WHO SMELLS
THAT'S WHAT THEY USED TO YELL
THEY'D SPRAY ME WITH LYSOL IN THE BACK STAIRWELL
TRIED SOAP
BUT NOPE
MY LIFE WAS A LIVING HELL
THAT SUMS IT UP IN A NUTSHELL
OH, WELL
I SMELL

TUG.

I WAS THE RUNNING BACK
UNTIL MY KNEES WENT CRACK
WOKE UP IN THE HOSPITAL – IT ALL WAS BLACK
MY KNEES
AH JEEZ
NO HEISMAN TROPHY, OR PAC-TEN PACK
MY LIFE TOOK A DIFFERENT TRACK
KNEES KEPT
ME BACK!

JOHNNY.

WANTED TO BE A STAR
BUT DIDN'T GET TOO FAR
ONLY GIGS IN A NIGHTCLUB WITH MY GUITAR
SOME PAY

JOHNNY. *(cont.)*
> I PLAY
> FROM FIVE TO SEVEN I'M THE STAR
> DOWNTOWN AT THE WONDER BAR
> WITH MY GUITAR

> *(**CALVIN**, **BUTCH**, **TUG**, and **JOHNNY** sing in a round.)*

CALVIN/BUTCH/JOHNNY.
> THAT'S WHO I WAS BACK THEN
> AND HERE WE ARE AGAIN
> HAVEN'T SEEN EACH OTHER SINCE GOD KNOWS WHEN,
> IT'S WRONG
> TOO LONG
> AS THICK AS THIEVES AND BEST OF FRIENDS
> PICKING UP WHERE WE LEFT OFF AGAIN
> FROM BOYS
> TO MEN
> REMEMBER ME?
> I WAS THE…

CALVIN.
> FUNNY GUY

BUTCH.
> BOY WHO SMELLS

TUG.
> RUNNING BACK

JOHNNY.
> MUSIC MAN

CALVIN/BUTCH/TUG/JOHNNY.
> WE'RE BACK WHERE IT BEGAN

> *(Everyone hugs and ad libs, catching up on the past thirty years. **BARBARA JEAN BEHLENDORF** enters. Back in high school she was the "easy girl.")*

BARBARA JEAN. Hi-hi! Remember me?

JOHNNY. Omigod, it's Barbara Jean Behlendorf!

CALVIN. *(sotto)* Ea-zay B. J.

> *(**TUG** and **CALVIN** high five. The **GIRLS** squeal and hug **BARBARA JEAN**.)*

DEBBIE. Omigod, Barbara Jean, you look exactly the same. Exactly.

BARBARA JEAN. I don't look too slutty, do I?

FRED "THE HEAD". Not to me.

BARBARA JEAN. Is that…Amy Aaron?

(They squeal and hug.)

What have you been doing all these years?

DEBBIE. *(speaking for her)* Nothing. Just raising kids.

(DEBBIE hands BARBARA JEAN a name tag.)

BARBARA JEAN. Do you have pictures?

(AMY flips open a long sheath of snapshots.)

AMY. That's Breanna. She just won a soccer scholarship to Notre Dame. My oldest, Trent. Pre-med UCLA. And my youngest, Henry. He's driving already. What about you?

(BARBARA JEAN reaches for her purse.)

BARBARA JEAN. One. My son. Preston. Here.

(BARBARA JEAN takes out a photo.)

DEBBIE. Oh, HE's gorgeous.

AMY. How old is he?

(BARBARA JEAN works up her courage.)

BARBARA JEAN. Thirty.

(The GIRLS react, perplexed.)

DEBBIE. Wow. He's 30 and…this is our 30th reunion. How is that mathematically possible?

BARBARA JEAN. Well…remember senior year when I was home for a couple of months with mono?

DEBBIE/AMY. Yes.

DEBBIE. Oh.

AMY. Oh!

DEBBIE. Oh.

BARBARA JEAN. Yeah.

AMY. How about that? May I see that picture again?

(**AMY** *subtly tries to look around and compare faces.*)

DEBBIE. Who's…? Who's the…?

BARBARA JEAN. Father? The truth is…I'm…not sure. It's the reason I'm here.

(Song: "IS IT YOU?")

TIMES WERE EASIER THEN
I KNOW I WAS
BUT NOW I'M HERE
MY MISSION'S CLEAR…
AND ALL BECAUSE…
(HE'S GOT) YOUR EYES OF BLUE
YOUR EYEBROWS TOO

BUT HE'S GOT HIS SMILE
HE'S GOT YOUR NOSE
YOUR CROOKED TOES
BUT HE'S GOT HIS SMILE
HE'S GOT YOUR HAIR
THAT DIMPLE THERE
THE SAME CROOKED FROWN
THAT MAKES HIS NOSTRILS FLARE
I SWEAR IT'S TRUE
IT COULD BE YOU
OR YOU

HE'S GOT YOUR VOICE
YOUR WARDROBE CHOICE
BUT HE'S GOT HIS SMILE
HE'S GOT YOUR STANCE
LOOKS THE SAME IN PANTS

BUT HE'S GOT HIS SMILE
HE'S GOT YOUR HEIGHT
LIKE YOU, HE'S BRIGHT
WHEN POLITICS COME UP
HE'S LEANS LIKE YOU – FAR RIGHT
I SWEAR IT'S TRUE
IT COULD BE YOU
OR YOU

I DON'T RECALL A SINGLE TIME
WHEN BOYS WEREN'T ON MY MIND
AND WHEN YOU'RE GOOD AT WHAT YOU DO
YOU'LL REALLY LOVE THAT DAILY GRIND
HE'S GOT YOUR SHRUG
YOUR BIG BEAR HUG

BUT HE'S GOT HIS SMILE
HE MOVES LIKE YOU
'S GOT BIG FEET, TOO
BUT HE'S GOT HIS SMILE
HE'S GOT YOUR KNEES
YOUR ALLERGIES
HE CAN'T EAT ANY SHELLFISH
AND HE CAN'T EAT CHEESE
WHAT A JAM I'M IN
IT COULD BE HIM
OR HIM

SEE, THERE WERE MORE THAN A FEW
SO TELL ME – WHAT DO I DO?
IT COULD BE YOU OR YOU OR YOU OR YOU.
OR HIM OR HIM.
OR YOU OR HIM OR YOU OR HIM?

(**JOHNNY** *starts handing out CDs.*)

JOHNNY. My new CD.

AMY. *(reading label)* "Johnny's Wine-Colored Tears."

JOHNNY. Track number two is my favorite. "Chardonnay, the Night, and You." See, there's this whole wine theme –

AMY. We get it.

(**MIKE** *looks over at* **SIMON**, *who points at himself.*)

SIMON. Simon Groupie.

MIKE TERZANO. I don't know what that means.

FRED "THE HEAD". *(to* **JOHNNY***)* Swear to God, man. Couple of years ago, I'm driving past the Keansburg Boardwalk and I see you standing on an egg crate in a pizza parlor with your guitar and a cup on the floor marked "tips."

JOHNNY. Oh, I was just helping out a friend.

FRED "THE HEAD". You never made it. Did you, man. Bummer.

(A series of flashbulbs go off, offstage. Ad lib excitement.)

Whoa…flashback.

DEBBIE. It's Bob Fields, everyone! Or should I say, Senator Bob Fields!

*(**SENATOR BOB FIELDS** enters with his wife **MARSHA**. During the following he gladhands everyone, pats backs, shakes hands, hands out BOB FIELDS CAMPAIGN BUTTONS. The lyrics never register with the people being insulted. They're too busy gazing in awe at Bob.)*

(Song: "I AM")

ALL.
  WHO'S THE MAN WE KNEW WOULD BE A SUCCESS?

BOB.
  I AM

ALL.
  WHO'S NAME DO WE DROP WHEN WE WANT TO IMPRESS?

BOB.
  MY NAME

ALL.
  WHO'S THE MAN BETTER THAN ALL OF THE REST
  AND SOMEDAY THE WHITE HOUSE MAY BE HIS ADDRESS?

BOB.
  IN CASE YOU DON'T KNOW – I WILL NOT MAKE YOU GUESS…
  I AM
  I AM
  WHO'S THE MAN YOU KNEW WOULD GO ALL THE WAY?

ALL.
  YOU ARE

BOB.
  WHO'S THE MAN YOU ASK TO BE WHEN YOU PRAY?

ALL.
  YOU ARE
  YOU ARE WHO

BOB.
>WHO IS YOUR FRIEND YOU'RE SO HAPPY TO SAY

ALL.
>WHOSE PROFILE WILL BE ON A QUARTER SOMEDAY?

BOB.
>THE MAN WITH THE GREAT SUITS?

CALVIN.
>AND LOUSY TOUPEE?

BOB. What?

ALL.
>YOU ARE

BOB/ALL.
>I AM/YOU ARE

ALL.
>BOB FIELDS HE'S THE ONE
>HE SHINES BRIGHTER THAN THE SUN
>YOU ME
>WE'RE ALL SLOBS
>WE SHOULD JUST THANK GOD
>THAT WE KNOW

WOMEN.
>BOB!

MEN.
>BOB BOB BOB BOB BOB BOB BOB BOB

BOB.
>WHO ARE THE PEOPLE WHO WON'T GET THIS FAR?

ALL.
>WE ARE

BOB.
>WHO IS EMBARRASSED CAUSE I SAW THEIR CAR?

ALL.
>WE ARE
>WE ARE WHO

BOB.
>WHO IS SO JEALOUS THAT I'M A BIG STAR?
>WHO HATES ME 'CAUSE I CAN BUY CAVIAR

ALL.
>AND NOW WHO IS GONNA GET DRUNK AT THE BAR?
>WE ARE
>WE ARE
>WE ARE
>WHO IS THE WOMAN TO WHOM HE IS WED?

MARSHA.
>I AM
>WHO'S SHAKEN HANDS 'TIL MY FINGERS HAVE BLED?

BOB.
>MARSHA
>MARSHA

MARSHA.
>WHO'LL STOP AT NOTHING TO GET HIM AHEAD?
>'TIL WE'RE IN THE WHITE HOUSE AND THE LINCOLN BED
>GET IN MY WAY AND I'LL SEE YOU ALL DEAD

ALL.
>MARSHA
>MARSHA

DEBBIE. Marsha, Marsha, Marsha.

BOB.
>WHO ARE THE PEOPLE I LEFT IN THE GRASS?

ALL.
>WE ARE
>WE ARE

BOB.
>WHO IS THE ONE YOU WILL NEVER SURPASS

ALL.
>YOU ARE
>YOU ARE

BOB.
>WHO MAKES YOU FEEL LIKE YOU'RE JUST SECOND CLASS
>WHO HAS THE BALLS THAT ARE MADE OUT OF BRASS?
>GO SCREW YOURSELVES YOU CAN ALL KISS MY ASS

ALL.
>YOU ARE
>YOU ARE

BOB.
>YOU ARE/I AM...!

DEBBIE. Hi, Mr. President. I know you're a Senator now, but you were OUR class president, so I called you president.

MARSHA. He doesn't mind.

BOB. Marsha, Debbie Policastro. Johnny Oches. Great musician. You still playing?

JOHNNY. Yes. In fact, I keep contacting your office about playing at your fundraisers, but I never hear back from you. Here's one of my CDs, "I See Your Face in My Beer."

MARSHA. I'll take that.

BOB. And this is Tug Fendermacher.

DEBBIE. He's our other class success story. Well, he would have been if he hadn't blown out his knee the first day of Dolphins' training camp and watched all his hopes and dreams turn to painkillers and booze.

TUG. Well, yes, I was crushed at first, but now I'm the marketing director for a big –

BOB. Hey. Failure's nothing to be ashamed of. Am I right, Johnny?

(**JOHNNY** *reacts.*)

TUG. Is there a bar in here?

(**TUG** *exits.*)

BOB. Say, speaking of "Successful," is Tommy Beekman here? Where is the "Most Likely to Succeed" famous doctor? Don't tell me, doing charity work for – what's his latest charity? – "Kids Without Bones?"

MARSHA. *(sotto)* Bob, you're a senator. You did great.

BOB. That's right. I did. My Facebook page is SO much better than his. Let's get in there before he shows up and tries to steal my thunder.

BOB. *(cont.)*
> WHO'S THE MAN YOU HAVE TO ADMIT
> MAKES YOU SO MAD YOU JUST WANT TO SPIT
> BECAUSE YOU ARE NOTHING AND I AM HOT SHIT

ALL.
> YOU ARE YOU ARE

BOB/ALL.
> I AM...!/YOU ARE...!

(The group exits to the gym.)

*(**TOMMY BEEKMAN** enters in an expensive suit. He calls off to someone behind him.)*

TOMMY. Come on, Christie, get the lead out.

*(**CHRISTIE** enters, in a long mink coat and a tiara.)*

CHRISTIE. You could wait for me, Tommy. It's not like we're in Japan.

TOMMY. Lucky for you, or the army and a lot of little helicopters would be trying to shoot you down.

CHRISTIE. It's 102 in here. It's June! Why do I have to wear this fur coat? I've got an open fire hydrant in my underpants!

TOMMY. Thanks for that visual.

*(**DEBBIE** sees them.)*

DEBBIE. Omigod! Homecoming Queen Christie O'Connor! You look...nice coat! And "Most Likely to Succeed" Tommy Beekman! Or should I say "Doctor" Beekman?"

TOMMY. Oh, come on. Just call me "Tommy."

(He looks around the hall.)

TOMMY. Like being home again, huh, Christie?

DEBBIE. We all feel like that.

TOMMY. No, I meant we have a hallway this large in our house.

DEBBIE. Oh. Have either of you seen Todd Finley?

TOMMY. Not unless he was driving my, you know, limo.

CHRISTIE. She gets it. You're loaded. Get the badges.

(**TOMMY** *goes to the sign-in table to get their badges.*)

CHRISTIE. *(to* **DEBBIE***)* Is, er…Julie Ryan showing up this year?

DEBBIE. She's supposed to.

(off **CHRISTIE***'s look)*

Oh, Christie. Don't you worry about how you look.

CHRISTIE. I wasn't.

DEBBIE. Are you nervous because you stole your best friend's boyfriend and now thirty years later she's coming back – divorced and successful and hot and you're afraid she might steal Tommy back?

(**DEBBIE** *has hit the nail on the head.*)

CHRISTIE. No.

DEBBIE. Then it's just because of the weight?

CHRISTIE. No!

DEBBIE. I'm going to go touch up my makeup. If Todd comes in while I'm gone…tell him you saw me, and I'm a total babe.

(**DEBBIE** *exits.* **TOMMY** *turns back with their name tags.*)

TOMMY. Here's your name tag. Hey, they put our senior pictures on them.

(**TOMMY** *goes to hand it to* **CHRISTIE**, *but stops to compare the old photo to his current wife.*)

Ooh.

CHRISTIE. I didn't know Julie Ryan was coming.

TOMMY. Oh. Is she?

(**TOMMY** *straightens his tie.*)

CHRISTIE. *(re: fur coat)* Is that what this is all about?

TOMMY. Of course not. You don't look any different with the coat off.

(**TOMMY** *adjusts his Rolex and rings so they shine better.*)

Now, let's get in there. And remember…

CHRISTIE. I know, I know. We're rich.

TOMMY. And don't you forget it. I was Most Likely to Succeed. They don't need to know we're...

(Song: "FAKING IT")

FAKING IT
FAKING IT
FAILURE IS MY NAME

CHRISTIE.

(HE'S A FLOP, HE'S A FLOP, HE'S A GIANT FLOP)

TOMMY/CHRISTIE.

FAKING IT

CHRISTIE.

(LOOK AT US FAKING IT)

TOMMY/CHRISTIE.

FAKING IT

CHRISTIE.

(THERE'S NO MISTAKING IT)

TOMMY/CHRISTIE.

AND EVERY YEAR THE SAME

(The music continues...)

CHRISTIE. Oh!oh!oh!oh!

TOMMY. Christie, what on earth are you doing?

CHRISTIE. What do you think I'm doing? I'm...

FAKING IT

TOMMY.

(WE HAVEN'T GOT A CENT)

TOMMY/CHRISTIE.

FAKING IT

CHRISTIE.

(WE CANNOT PAY THE RENT)

TOMMY/CHRISTIE.

NO ONE HAS A CLUE

TOMMY.

(THERE'S NO DOUGH, THERE'S NO DOUGH, THERE'S NO DOUGH-DEE-OO)

TOMMY/CHRISTIE.

FAKING IT

TOMMY.
(WE HAVEN'T GOT A DIME)
TOMMY/CHRISTIE.
FAKING IT
CHRISTIE.
(THIS BRA'S NOT EVEN MINE)
TOMMY/CHRISTIE.
THAT'S WHAT WE'RE GONNA DO

(They dance, shimmying etc. Suddenly **TOMMY** *tap dances wildly.)*

CHRISTIE. Tommy. You don't dance. What are you doing?
TOMMY. What do you think I'm doing? I'm…
FAKING IT
CHRISTIE.
(WE LOST IT ALL IN STOCKS!)
TOMMY.
FAKING IT
CHRISTIE.
(OUR NEXT HOUSE IS A BOX!)
TOMMY/CHRISTIE.
HELP US FROM THIS PIT
(IT'S THE PITS, IT'S THE PITS, IT'S THE STINKIN' PITS)
FAKING IT
TOMMY.
(SOMEDAY WE'RE CLIMBING OUT!)
TOMMY/CHRISTIE.
FAKING IT
CHRISTIE.
('TIL THEN THERE IS NO DOUBT!)
TOMMY/CHRISTIE.
THAT WE'LL FAKING
THAT WE'LL BE FAKING
THAT WE'LL BE FAKING IT
(THEY'LL NEVER KNOW THAT WE'LL BE FAKING IT)

(blackout)

Scene Three

(SETTING: Girls' room)

(AT RISE: Stalls are upstage. A bank of sinks sit downstage. **DEBBIE** *and* **AMY** *stare into the imaginary downstage mirror.)*

DEBBIE. You know, I think everyone's here that RSVP'd except for Todd and Julie Ryan. Do you think that means Todd's not coming?

AMY. Debbie, people are coming from all over. It's not like we all live in town anymore.

DEBBIE. Just you.

*(***CHRISTIE*** enters.)*

CHRISTIE. Wow. This is weird. I've never been in here without a cigarette.

AMY. Aren't you hot?

CHRISTIE. It's not so bad.

*(***CHRISTIE*** reaches under her fur coat and wipes under her arms with a paper towel and wrings it out in the sink. The other girls pretend not to see.)*

AMY. Hey, did you hear? Barbara Jean has a son! And doesn't know who the father is.

CHRISTIE. What a slut. She came on to my father once at the hardware store. That's why we stopped being friends.

*(***BARBARA JEAN*** enters.)*

BARBARA JEAN. Hi, girls.

(Happy ad lib hellos.)

DEBBIE. Hey there, little mother.

BARBARA JEAN. I can't believe we're all back in the girls' room again.

DEBBIE. Is he here yet?

BARBARA JEAN. Who?

DEBBIE. Todd! Who do you think? If he doesn't show up then this whole night is just useless.

BARBARA JEAN. *(smacking her forehead)* Todd!

*(**BARBARA JEAN** scribbles his name in her little book. **DEBBIE** doesn't catch it. **AMY** does.)*

CHRISTIE. You know the only thing better than seeing you guys tonight? NOT seeing Julie Ryan.

AMY. She's a big New York magazine editor. She's too important to come to this.

DEBBIE. She just got divorced. I bet she comes.

BARBARA JEAN. She's divorced?

CHRISTIE. Of course she is. Who could live with her?

(Song: "CONCEITED BITCH POLKA")

ALL.
SHE WAS THE ONE
WHO COULD DO NOTHING WRONG
TO LITTLE MISS PERFECT
WE DEDICATE THIS SONG
VOTED MOST POPULAR
HEAD CHEERLEADER TOO
SHE NEVER ATE
HER HAIR WAS STRAIGHT
IF YOU KNEW HER YOU'D HATE HER TOO
EVERYTHING CAME EASY
SHE WAS CUTE AND RICH
SHE WAS A STUCK UP
CONCEITED
STUCK UP
CONCEITED
STUCK UP
CONCEITED
BITCH
MADE THE HONOR ROLL
ON EVERY TEST AN "A"
TEACHER'S PET
AND EVERY BOY'S DREAM LAY

BE THANKFUL WHEN SHE GRANTS A SMILE
BE SURE TO MAKE A FUSS
EYES BIG AND BLUE
SHE'S STILL SIZE TWO

CHRISTIE.
NOT SIZE TWELVE OR FOURTEEN LIKE US!

(The others shoot her a look.)

ALL.
EVERYTHING CAME EASY
SHE WAS CUTE AND RICH
SHE WAS A STUCK UP
CONCEITED
STUCK UP
CONCEITED
STUCK UP
CONCEITED
BITCH

DEBBIE.
AROUND THE TOWN SHE'D STRUT

BARBARA JEAN.
LIKE SHE'D HUNG THE MOON

AMY.
WE HATE HER SKINNY GUTS

CHRISTIE.
DOES SHE THINKS SHE PEES PERFUME?

ALL.
SHE NEVER HAD ZITS
WHILE WE SQUEEZED AND POKED
THE ONE THE BOYS LOVED
THAT WE ALL WANTED TO CHOKE
SHE HAD A CHARMED LIFE
WE HAVE TO AGREE
I'D LIKE TO KICK HER ASS
'CAUSE THAT SHOULD HAVE BEEN ME
OH WE STILL HATE HER
CAUSE OUR BOYFRIENDS
WANTED TO DATE HER

SHE WAS A STUCK UP
CONCEITED
STUCK UP
CONCEITED
STUCK UP…
CONCEITED

(CHRISTIE scribbles "Bitch" on the mirror with her lipstick.)

ALL. *(cont.)*
BITCH
A BITCH!

(DEBBIE drags CHRISTIE by the arm and they exit. After a beat, the bathroom stall door opens, and JULIE steps out.)

JULIE. And I'M the bitch?

(blackout)

Scene Four

*(**SETTING**: The gym. The gym is decorated to celebrate the "Class of '79." Two large round tables with centerpieces.)*

*(**AT RISE**: The crowd dances to an instrumental disco song.)*

(Song: "SHOW YOUR MUSCLE")

ALL.
SHOW YOUR MUSCLES
SHOW YOUR MUSCLES
SHOW YOUR MUSCLES

*(The song ends, people part and take their seats at the same table on one side of the room – revealing **BUTCH** sitting alone at the other.)*

BUTCH. Oh, come on.

*(Lights up on **JOHNNY** and **TUG**.)*

JOHNNY. You know who my favorite band was?

TUG. No. I have no idea who your favorite band was.

JOHNNY. Guess Who.

TUG. Springsteen?

JOHNNY. No. Guess Who.

TUG. Pink Floyd?

JOHNNY. Guess Who.

TUG. I give up.

JOHNNY. What do you mean?

TUG. I have no idea who your favorite band was.

JOHNNY. I just told you who it was. Guess Who.

TUG. Who.

JOHNNY. No. Guess Who.

TUG. Guess who?

JOHNNY. Yes.

TUG. Oh. Your favorite band is Yes?

JOHNNY. No. Guess Who.

TUG. Who?

JOHNNY. Guess Who. The band.

TUG. Oh, the Band? Yeah. "Last Waltz" was great.

JOHNNY. Not The Band. Guess Who.

TUG. I have no idea.

JOHNNY. No idea about what?

TUG. Guess who.

JOHNNY. Yes.

TUG. That's what I thought. Yes.

JOHNNY. No. Not Yes.

TUG. Not Yes. Not the Band. Then Who?

JOHNNY. No. Not them either.

TUG. You know what? Go screw yourself.

(FRED walks up carrying a plate of food.)

FRED "THE HEAD". Meatloaf?

JOHNNY. No, but he was good, too.

(Lights up on AMY and MIKE TERZANO.)

MIKE TERZANO. *(reading her name tag)* Amy Aaron. You delectable beauty. And what a beautiful dress. It will look so great on my floor.

AMY. What?

MIKE TERZANO. Debbie told me you married...

AMY. Chuck Murdock.

MIKE TERZANO. Chuck Murdock. Damn him. He always was my arch nemesis.

AMY. He didn't go to school with us. How could he be your arch nemesis?

MIKE TERZANO. He married the love of my life, didn't he? Say, where is old Chuck?

AMY. Oh, he passed away.

MIKE TERZANO. Really. That's too bad.

(Behind her back he makes victory motions. She almost catches him. Big laughter from the other side of the room. CALVIN's in the middle of a joke.)

CALVIN. "Don't look now – this one's eating my popcorn!"

(More laughter. **CALVIN** *sees every school boy's fantasy* **MISS BLUMQUIST**, *the hot teacher from 1979, speaking with* **DEBBIE**.*)*

CALVIN. Oh, sweet Jesus, she's still here.

BUTCH. Who?

*(***MISS BLUMQUIST*** approaches.)*

MISS BLUMQUIST. Hello, boys.

BOYS. Hello, Miss Blumquist.

MISS BLUMQUIST. You all remember me?

BOYS. Do we?!!

MISS BLUMQUIST. My, Calvin Giblin. Have you grown up.

CALVIN. Yes, yes I have, Miss Blumquist.

MISS BLUMQUIST. You always were one of my favorites.

CALVIN. Well…Spank me, spank you, thank you.

MISS BLUMQUIST. Nice to see you.

*(***MISS BLUMQUIST*** talks to the next table.* **BUTCH** *studies* **CALVIN***, who is in a trance.)*

BUTCH. What's wrong, Calvin?

(Song: "MISS BLUNQUIST")

CALVIN.
WHEN I WAS ALL ALONE
MY HEAD AGAINST MY PILLOW
I'D THINK OF MISS BLUMQUIST
WHILE GAZING AT MY WILLOW
THE ANGEL OF MY YOUTH
I DREAM OF HER TO THIS DAY…
SO JUST BETWEEN THE TWO OF US
THERE'S ONE THING I MUST SAY…
I WANT TO BANG MISS BLUMQUIST
I WANT TO BANG HER HARD
INSIDE AN EMPTY CLASSROOM
OUT IN THE OLD SCHOOL YARD

CALVIN. *(cont.)* Calvin Giblin reporting for detention. I've been a bad boy.
I WANT TO BANG MISS BLUMQUIST
I WANT TO MAKE HER SHOUT
I WANT TO BANG MISS BLUMQUIST
UNTIL WE BOTH PASS OUT
ON HER DESK
ON HER CHAIR
TIL SHE GRABS ME BY THE HAIR
WITH A POINTER AND A MAP
WE'LL MAKE HISTORY ON MY LAP
IN THE FOUNTAIN WHERE IT'S WET
I WILL HEAR HER SCREAM 'NOT YET'
IN THE GYM BY THE GATE
I WILL YELL BACK "IT'S TOO LATE!"
EVERY MINUTE IT GROWS STRONGER
I CAN'T HOLD BACK ANY LONGER
SHE IS TALKING SENTENCE STRUCTURE
DOES SHE KNOW I'M GONNA RUPTURE?

(**CALVIN** *howls as he leaps up on the table.*)

Here I come, Miss Blumquist. I'm gonna polish your apple.
I WANT TO BANG MISS BLUMQUIST
WE'RE GONNA BUMP AND GRIND
I WANT TO BANG MISS BLUMQUIST
I'M GONNA BANG HER BLIND

I dream of you Miss Blumquist. Do you dream of me, too? Come take my hand, Miss Blumquist. Let's make our dreams come true.

I DREAM OF YOU MISS BLUMQUIST
IT'S ALWAYS BEEN JUST YOU
OH, PLEASE SAY YES, MISS BLUMQUIST
YOU'LL SEE HOW MUCH I GREW...!

MISS BLUMQUIST. Calvin, get down from there. You aren't too old to be punished, you know.

CALVIN. Yes. Yes, I know.

(Lights up on SIMON and BARBARA JEAN.)

SIMON. Hi, Barbara Jean. It's me. Simon Groupie.

BARBARA JEAN. I'm sorry. Did you say something to me?

SIMON. Yes. I'm speaking to you right now. I know I don't make the strongest of impressions. If you'll recall, I never missed a day of school in my life, yet in my junior year I was marked absent 93 times. But things are going to be different now. I've had a lot of therapy since high school. In fact, it was my therapist who insisted I come back here. To prove that I'm as important as anyone here. We're not who we were in high school. What matters is who we are now. And I'm a valuable worthwhile human being.

BARBARA JEAN. I'm sorry. Are you talking to me?

SIMON. Uh…no. Sorry.

(SIMON walks away.)

(TOMMY enters.)

BOB. Tommy!

TOMMY. Bobby!

(They hug.)

BOB. Marsha, this is Tommy Beekman.

MARSHA. Oh, I've heard so much about you.

BOB. I hear from Debbie's alumni newsletter that you've done okay for yourself. Head of surgery at NYU. Doctors Without Borders. Took in all those Katrina victims. Guess you deserved "Most Likely to Succeed."

TOMMY. I do what I can.

BOB. Yeah? Well, care to help out an old friend with a campaign contribution?

MARSHA. Bob. He's incorrigible. Can you?

(TOMMY hesitates.)

TOMMY. Oh. Sure. Put me down for…250.

BOB. 250? Marsha, can you believe this guy? You can't donate more than 37 hundred in this state, Tommy. You want me to go to jail?

(**CHRISTIE** *approaches with a plate of food.*)

You believe this, everybody? Tommy tried to give me $250,000.

(**CHRISTIE** *chokes on her food.*)

CHRISTIE. You what?

BOB. Omigod. Is that Christie? Christie!

(**CHRISTIE** *and* **BOB** *hug.*)

MARSHA. Hello. I'm Marsha. It's so nice to meet Bob's old friends.

CHRISTIE. So nice to meet the girl who married Bob. We all had such a crush on him. Class president. Starred in all the school plays. Quarterback for the football team. King of the Prom. And accepted into Harvard in his junior year.

BOB. Yet, not voted Most Likely to Succeed. Go figure.

TOMMY. Hey. What can I say? I'm lucky. Voted "Most Likely to Succeed" AND got the Homecoming Queen.

CHRISTIE. Whoa. Stand back. Those pigs in a blanket are going right through me. Want to come to the ladies room with me, Marsha?

MARSHA. Not really.

BOB. Marsha. She's a voter.

(**MARSHA** *moans a little but does her duty.* **CHRISTIE** *and* **MARSHA** *exit.*)

(**TUG** *races in.*)

CALVIN. Tug, are you all right? You look like you've seen a ghost.

TUG. I think I have. She's here!

TOMMY. Who's here?

MEN. Julie!

JOHNNY. Told you she'd be here. Divorcees always show up.

(**BUTCH**, **FRED** *and* **JOHNNY** *exchange money.*)

CALVIN. You still have a thing for her?

TUG. Who doesn't?

(Song: "JULIE")

ALL.
>WHO BROKE OUR HEARTS
>AND WHO WOULD WE GLADLY HAVE HER
>BREAK THEM AGAIN?
>JULIE
>JULIE
>
>WHO DROVE US WILD
>WITH HER DAZZLING SMILE UNTIL WE
>ALL WERE ACHIN'
>IT'S JULIE
>JULIE
>
>WHO DID WE PRAY WOULD TURN INTO A NYMPHOMANIAC?
>WHO'S GOT THE EYES OF A GODDESS – NOT TO MENTION
>   THE RACK?
>JACK
>JULIE
>JULIE

FRED "THE HEAD".
>FOR YOU I'D EVEN SELL CRACK…

MEN.
>WHO MADE OUR DAYS
>AND ALL OF OUR NIGHTS
>AS BRIGHT AS A MORNING SUN?
>JULIE
>JULIE
>
>WHO DO WE PICTURE
>WHEN WE HAVE SEX WITH OUR WIVES
>UNTIL IT'S DONE?
>JULIE
>JULIE
>JULIE

MEN. *(cont.)*
>WHO DO WE MORE THAN ANYONE WANT RIGHT HERE IN OUR LAP?
>WHO DO WE STILL THINK OF – WHENEVER WE NAP?
>CHAP
>WHO MADE OUR DAYS
>AND ALL OF OUR NIGHTS
>AS BRIGHT AS A MORNING SUN?
>IT'S JULIE
>JULIE
>JULIE
>JULIE
>NEXT TO YOU OUR WIVES LOOK LIKE CRAP.
>LIKE CRAP!
>JULIE...!

JULIE. Hi, Guys. Been a long time. Good to see you!

>(**JULIE** *takes in the room. People part as she crosses downstage.*)

TUG. Hi, Julie.

JULIE. Hi, Tug.

>(**JULIE** *hugs him.*)

BUTCH. Hi, Julie.

JULIE. Hi, Butch. You smell nice.

>(**JULIE** *takes his hand.*)

BUTCH. Thank you.

SIMON. Hi, Julie.

>(**JULIE** *passes right past* **SIMON** *and zeroes in on* **TOMMY**.*)*

JULIE. Hello, Tommy.

TOMMY. Hello, Julie. Wow, you look great.

JULIE. You do, too. How are you doing?

>(**CHRISTIE** *and* **MARSHA** *return from the ladies room.*)

CHRISTIE. Julie Ryan. So sorry to hear about your divorce. It must be so horrible knowing your husband left you for a much younger woman. She was your cleaning lady, right?

JULIE. Do I know you?

(excited)

Omigod, I'd recognize you anywhere. You must be Christie's mother.

FRED. Oh, no she di-'nt

(TUG returns with a drink. He offers it to JULIE.)

TUG. Drink?

TOMMY. Thank you.

(TOMMY downs it. He hands TUG the empty glass.)

CHRISTIE. *(motions JULIE closer)* Oh, Julie? You have a little…

(CHRISTIE motions to her chin.)

JULIE. A little what?

CHRISTIE. I'm not sure what it is. Might be vomit from your most recent purge.

(Reaction from the crowd.)

JULIE. See that? You CAN get laughs from the front.

(Reaction from the crowd.)

What? I didn't shove the Krispy Kremes down her throat.

(She wins. JULIE walks away.)

BARBARA JEAN. God, she hasn't changed at all.

CHRISTIE. What a bitch.

MARSHA. *(to BOB)* Omigod. Were they always like this?

BOB. Actually Julie and Christie were best friends until Christie stole Tommy.

MARSHA. Tommy picked Christie over Julie?

BOB. Yeah. And yet they voted him "Most Likely to…"

MARSHA. Oh, give it a rest.

(**JOHNNY** *approaches* **DEBBIE**.)

JOHNNY. Debbie, I noticed the music stopped. Would you like me to get up and sing a –

DEBBIE. No. Sit down.

(**MISS BLUMQUIST** *takes the dance floor with a microphone.*)

MISS BLUMQUIST. Take your seats, everybody. We thought it would be fun to read the predictions you made in your senior year of where you thought you'd be today.

(Ad lib excitement.)

These been under lock and key for thirty years by your old guidance counselor – Mr. Stinitski.

(**BARBARA JEAN** *does a spit take.*)

BARBARA JEAN. Stinitski?! Forgot about him.

(**BARBARA JEAN** *writes his name in her book.*)

AMY. Jeez Louise.

(Underscore: "NO WAY TO KNOW")

MISS BLUMQUIST. He wanted to be with us tonight but…as luck would have it – American Doll Convention, same weekend. Anyway, let's start with…Simon Groupie? Sorry, that must be from a different class. Here's one. Fred "the Head" Colicchio?

(**SIMON** *sits.*)

(reads from card) Fred thought he'd be…"Growing pot on my legal-by-now pot ranch for Sunkist."

(People laugh.)

FRED "THE HEAD". The wheels of change spin slowly, my friends.

(**MISS BLUMQUIST** *takes another card.*)

MISS BLUMQUIST. Amy Aaron…

(**AMY** *stands and waves.*)

MISS BLUMQUIST. *(cont.) (reads card)* …was going to be a doctor and cure cancer. How'd that work out for you, Amy?

CALVIN. Show him your kids' pictures.

(Laughter. **AMY** *sits in defeat.)*

MISS BLUMQUIST. Tommy Beekman – Most Likely to Succeed.

BOB. Did he top being a Senator? I don't think so.

MARSHA. Bob. Sit down.

(He does.)

TOMMY. I hope the light reflecting off my Rolex doesn't blind him while he's reading.

MISS BLUMQUIST. *(reads from card)* Tommy's prediction: "Wherever I am thirty years from now, no matter how much I accomplish I'll be a winner. Because I'll still be with the love of my life…

*(***CHRISTIE** *takes* **TOMMY***'s hand as people "ahh.")*

…Julie Ryan."

(An awkward response from the crowd. **CHRISTIE** *pulls back her hand.* **JULIE** *is equally stunned.)*

TOMMY. I wrote that before you and I –

*(***CHRISTIE** *continues silently yelling at him. Music ends.)*

MISS BLUMQUIST. Um…let's…take a break and read a few more of these later.

(handing mic to **DEBBIE***)*

Well, that sucked.

DEBBIE. Ssh. Your mic is still on.

*(***TODD FINLEY** *enters.)*

(accidentally into the mic) Omigod. Look who it is, everybody!

*(***DEBBIE** *shoves the microphone at* **BLUMQUIST** *and bolts towards* **TODD***. Ad lib hellos.)*

JOHNNY. How are you, Todd?

TODD. Great. Sorry I'm late, I got lost. Did you know Woolworth's is a Restoration Hardware now?

DEBBIE. Stop hogging him. He just got here! Here's your table, Todd. Get up, Butch.

*(**DEBBIE** manhandles **TODD** and directs him to the best table. **BUTCH** gets out of "Todd's" seat. **DEBBIE** steals the chair next to him for herself, unaware **SIMON** was about to sit in it.)*

Can I get you anything, Todd?

TODD. No, I'm good.

DEBBIE. You look good. I heard about the divorce. Are you okay?

TODD. I'm great. Remarkably great. It's just so good to be free, you know? I'm free now!

DEBBIE. That is great.

*(**DEBBIE** moves a hair closer. **TODD** looks at **DEBBIE**. She gets slightly embarrassed by the way he's looking.)*

TODD. You know, Debbie, you were the only one who really "got" me in high school. All the times we'd stay on the phone talking all night. Or hanging out in your basement listening to Billy Joel records and talking about the future. I've spent the last thirty years looking for something like what we had.

DEBBIE. Really? Oh, Todd.

*(**SIMON** comes between **DEBBIE** and **TODD**, halting their conversation. They stare at him and he slowly walks away. **JULIE** approaches **TOMMY**. **CHRISTIE** is not there.)*

JULIE. Tommy? You really thought you'd spend the rest of your life with me?

TOMMY. Yes, but to be fair, back then I also thought I could get girls by wearing yellow velour pants. Hey, I'm sorry about what Christie said before. She didn't mean it. She's just insecure.

JULIE. Where is she?

TOMMY. I don't know. Probably getting cake.

JULIE. Somehow I thought it would be different coming back this time. I'm older. I'm divorced. There's nothing for them to be jealous about anymore.

TOMMY. I don't know about that.

JULIE. You know, this is the first time we spoken since the night I found you with Christie in the back of the music room.

TOMMY. Yeah, I was going to call you…but I didn't know what to say. Let's face it. I was an immature jerk back then.

*(**CHRISTIE** enters.)*

Gotta go.

*(**TOMMY** runs to her. **JULIE** exits outside in the opposite direction.)*

CHRISTIE. Cake?

TOMMY. I'm good.

*(**TOMMY** pulls out a chair for **CHRISTIE**. She sits. **DEBBIE** takes the dance floor with the microphone.)*

DEBBIE. Attention, everyone. Attention, everyone. Stop talking Bob and Butch.

TOMMY. I'll be right back.

*(**TOMMY** exits. **TUG** grabs the microphone from **DEBBIE**.)*

TUG. All Vikings, please report to the football field. All Vikings, please report to the football field.

*(**DEBBIE** tries to get the microphone back.)*

DEBBIE. What are you doing, Tug?

TUG. We all remember that great division championship game December 2nd 1978. When Tug Fendermacher made the winning touchdown! Well, let's get out there and relive the greatness!

(No one moves.)

Outside. Now.

(People start to get up and head for the football field.)

DEBBIE. Give me the mic, Tug.

*(**DEBBIE** and **TUG** struggle for the microphone.)*

TUG. *(into mic)* What say we do it for old time's sake? Vikings!!!

(More people head for the door.)

DEBBIE. No going outside. It's time for the dance-off.

*(No one listens to **DEBBIE**. Everyone exits to the football field.)*

JOHNNY. Do you want me to sing a –

DEBBIE. No. Get out of here, Johnny.

*(**DEBBIE** realizes she's now alone with **TODD**.)*

Todd?

TUG. Let's go, Todd!

TODD. Vikings rule!

*(**TODD** leaves **DEBBIE** and runs off. **DEBBIE** sighs.)*

DEBBIE. He's really here!

(Song: "BACK IN HIGH SCHOOL (REPRISE)")

THIS NIGHT COULD BE MY LAST CHANCE
FOR TODD AND OUR TRUE ROMANCE
I AM BACK IN HIGH SCHOOL!

(blackout)

Scene Five

(*SETTING: Football field*)

(*AT RISE:* **JULIE** *is alone on the field in the moonlight.*)

(Song: "GARDEN STATE OF MIND")

JULIE.
THE OLD "BROAD STREET SODA SHOPPE" IS GONE
OUR BIKE PATH IS A "BED BATH AND BEYOND"
AND THEY BUILT CONDOS ON BROOKDALE POND
SO I GUESS IT'S TRUE WHAT THEY SAY
TIME MARCHES ON

"WOOLWORTH'S" IS NOW "RESTORATION HARDWARE"
THERE'S ASSISTED LIVING WHERE WE HELD OUR TOWN FAIR
YET I'M STILL HERE SEARCHING FOR WHO I WAS BACK THERE
IF EVERYTHING'S CHANGED…
HOW DO I FIND ME ANYWHERE?

LITTLE BRIDGE ROAD IS THREE LANES WIDE
THERE'S A GIANT STRIP MALL ON THE OTHER SIDE
WHEN I THINK OF ALL THE NIGHTS I HAVE CRIED
HOW DO I REBUILD ME?
GOD KNOWS I'VE TRIED
OH HOW I'VE TRIED

THERE'S A "STARBUCKS" IN MY SAVINGS AND LOAN
SCENIC DRIVE IS A NO-PARKING ZONE
MAYBE IF I FOUND SOMEONE TO CALL MY OWN
THEN I'D FEEL LIKE I'VE COME HOME

AND WE'LL DRIVE DOWN OAK STREET
WHERE THEY CUT DOWN ALL THE TREES
WE'LL PASS MY OLD HOUSE – WHICH IS NOW A CHUCK E. CHEESE
AND HE'LL TURN TO ME AND ASK "WHAT'S WITH ALL THE VIETNAMESE?"

JULIE. *(cont.)*
AND I WON'T CARE 'CAUSE I FOUND THE MAN I CAN TRUST
AS WE DRIVE OFF INTO THE SUNSET PAST THAT GIANT TOYS R US
OUR DRIVE-IN MOVIE IS NOW A BIG "COST-CO"
WHERE WE MADE OUT THEY SELL JUMBO JARS OF BOSCO
SO TELL ME, IF A WHOLE TOWN CAN CHANGE AND GROW
WHY CAN'T I?
PLEASE, SOMEONE LET ME KNOW!

*(**TOMMY** joins her, attempting to look like he just bumped into her. **JULIE** drains her glass of champagne and sets it down. They are both very nervous.)*

TOMMY. God, it's so weird to be back here.

JULIE. Everybody looks so different.

TOMMY. Can you believe it? Johnny lost all his hair.

(beat)

JULIE. Amy's kids are so cute.

(beat)

TOMMY. They really are.

*(Beat. Then **JULIE** and **TOMMY** jump on each other making out like crazy.)*

JULIE. Stop. Wait a minute. What are we doing?

TOMMY. I know. I'm married. She could take half my wealth. I don't want to go into numbers, but they're, you know, really up there….

JULIE. So what? I knew you when you had nothing.

TOMMY. Yeah, well…

JULIE. Back when we had our whole lives ahead of us. Anything was possible.

TOMMY. Yeah. Before I ruined everything.

JULIE. SHE ruined everything. She stole you from me. If only we could go back and fix all our mistakes.

*(**JULIE** tears up and falls into his arms. **TOMMY** pats her back. She leans up. They look at each other and then they go in for a kiss.)*

(Stadium lights go on full.)

(JULIE and TOMMY jump apart. His arms fly up in the air out of nerves.)

TOMMY. Ya! Touchdown!

(The classmates walk out onto the football field for the first time in thirty years. The guys wear football jerseys. TUG carries a box.)

BARBARA JEAN. How'd you guys get out here so fast?

TOMMY. What's with all the questions! Jesus Christ. Go have another baby, why don't you!

(The others walk out on the field.)

TUG. Wow. Feels good to be back here.

MIKE TERZANO. It really does. The old field. The old sod. The old athletic grounds.

JOHNNY. Looks a lot smaller than the last time I saw it.

CALVIN. That's what she said.

(big laughs)

JOHNNY. You know, I wrote a song about our games out here. It was on my second album, "A Scotch-Colored Morning."

(JOHNNY pulls out his guitar.)

TUG. Johnny, please. We're on a football field. If we wanted to hear music, we'd ask Barbara Jean to strap on her old clarinet.

(TUG hands TOMMY a jersey.)

JULIE. Hey, Amy. You remember this?

(JULIE does a cheer.)

Three cheers for old Lincroft High.

(DEBBIE, AMY, CHRISTIE, and BARBARA JEAN join in.)

GIRLS. You bring the whisky. I'll bring the rye. When we yell, we yell like hell for the glory of Lincroft High!

(**JULIE** *ends with a cartwheel. The others do their best, but can't manage the old moves.*)

CALVIN. Thank you for that. Excuse me, I have to go change my pants.

CHRISTIE. Christ, something just popped and is hanging down my leg.

TUG. Hey, look what I found.

(**TUG** *shows a football.*)

CALVIN. Is that?

TUG. THE game ball.

TODD. He brought it with him?

BUTCH. He broke the display case.

TUG. Hey, guys. Remember what Coach Bell always said before every game?

SIMON. "Who are you and what are you doing in the locker room?"

(*Everyone looks at him, then turns back.*)

TUG. Before every game…

(Song: "DON'T DROP THE BALL")

MY COACH SAID
DON'T DROP, DON'T DROP, DON'T DROP, DON'T DROP THE BALL
YES, HE SAID
DON'T DROP, DON'T DROP, DON'T DROP, DON'T DROP THE BALL
HE TOLD ME
DON'T DROP, DON'T DROP, DON'T DROP, DON'T DROP THE BALL
I HEARD HIM
DON'T DROP, DON'T DROP, DON'T DROP, DON'T DROP THE BALL
YES, COACH SAID
DON'T DROP, DON'T DROP, DON'T DROP, DON'T DROP THE BALL
EACH PRACTICE
DON'T DROP, DON'T DROP, DON'T DROP, DON'T DROP THE BALL
AT PEP TALKS
DON'T DROP, DON'T DROP, DON'T DROP, DON'T DROP THE BALL
FROM THE SIDELINES
DON'T DROP, DON'T DROP, DON'T DROP, DON'T DROP THE BALL

IN THE FINAL GAME
THERE WAS NO TIME ON THE CLOCK
THE PLAY WAS "HAIL MARY"
IF OUR TEAM COULD ONLY BLOCK
WE WERE DOWN BY FIVE
IT WAS ALL UP TO ME
TO GET THE BALL I'D DIVE
IF THAT'S HOW IT HAD TO BE
I GRABBED THAT BALL
I STILL DON'T KNOW FROM WHERE
I DUG DEEP DOWN
AND I RAN FAST SUCKING AIR
IF I CROSSED THAT LINE
I COULD WIN IT FOR THE TEAM
THE CROWD STOOD UP
AND I HEARD THEM START TO SCREAM
BUT IT WASN'T "DO IT, TUG!"
OR EVEN "GO FOR THE GOLD."
CAUSE ALL I HEARD WAS WHAT I'D BEEN ALWAYS TOLD...
THEY YELLED OUT
DON'T DROP, DON'T DROP, DON'T DROP, DON'T DROP THE BALL
LIKE MY COACH SAID
DON'T DROP, DON'T DROP, DON'T DROP, DON'T DROP THE BALL
FOSHIZZLE
DON'T DROP, DON'T DROP, DON'T DROP, DON'T DROP THE BALL
GET JIGGY
DON'T DROP, DON'T DROP, DON'T DROP, DON'T DROP THE BALL
MY COACH SAID
DON'T DROP, DON'T DROP, DON'T DROP, DON'T DROP THE BALL
I HEARD IT
DON'T DROP, DON'T DROP, DON'T DROP, DON'T DROP THE BALL
THEY ALL YELLED
DON'T DROP, DON'T DROP, DON'T DROP, DON'T DROP THE BALL
CAN YOU DIG IT?
DON'T DROP, DON'T DROP, DON'T DROP, DON'T DROP THE BALL

Boyee!

(spoken)

So I didn't.

JULIE. And Tug's catch won us the state championship! Go Vikings!

TUG. Greatest game of my life. Remember…Bob, you were quarterback. Can't remember who it was, but someone was blocking for me….

SIMON. That was me.

(TUG stares at SIMON for a beat. He's never seen him before.)

TUG. Let's re-live it.

JOHNNY. What, now?

TUG. Yeah. Come on. What do you say?

BUTCH. Sure.

BOB. Why not?

MIKE TERZANO. Same old positions, let's go.

(The guys are lined up to recreate the play.)

CALVIN. *(taking position as Center)* Are any of you proctologists? Might as well kill two birds.

TUG. Butch, you remember what to do on this play?

BUTCH. I don't smell anymore –

TUG. I don't care. The other team doesn't know that. Just do it.

BUTCH. Other team? We're playing ourselves.

FRED "THE HEAD". Just do it, man, so we can all go back inside.

(BUTCH sighs, then raises his armpits up on the line.)

BOB. Blue 32. Green 19. Green 19. Hike.

(Lighting change. During the following the guys run down field "in SLO-MO" and pretend to block, as TUG runs and BOB passes him the ball. BUTCH holds up arms up and tries to torture the other imaginary team with the odor from under his arms as TUG "runs" behind him towards the goal. One by one the entire team goes down, except for TUG who runs the ball in.)

LADIES.
> REMEMBER
> DON'T DROP, DON'T DROP, DON'T DROP, DON'T DROP THE BALL

AMY.
> HANG ON, TUG!

LADIES.
> DON'T DROP, DON'T DROP, DON'T DROP, DON'T DROP THE BALL

DEBBIE.
> ALL THE WAY, TUG!

LADIES.
> DON'T DROP, DON'T DROP, DON'T DROP, DON'T DROP THE BALL

CHRISTIE.
> IT'S YOUR BIRTHDAY!

LADIES.
> DON'T DROP, DON'T DROP, DON'T DROP, DON'T DROP THE BALL

MARSHA.
> I GOT NOTHING

LADIES.
> DON'T DROP, DON'T DROP, DON'T DROP, DON'T DROP THE BALL

JULIE.
> WATCH HIM GO, NOW

LADIES.
> DON'T DROP, DON'T DROP, DON'T DROP, DON'T DROP THE BALL

BARBARA JEAN.
> MY SON'S AN ATHLETE!

*(**BARBARA JEAN** scribbles in her book.)*

ALL.
> DON'T DROP, DON'T DROP, DON'T DROP, DON'T DROP THE BALL
> DON'T DROP, DON'T DROP, DON'T DROP, DON'T DROP THE BALL

(The girls cheer. The lights restore. The entire "TEAM" is spread out on the field like the wounded on a battlefield. They groan.)

TOMMY. My back!

JOHNNY. My leg!

BOB. I can't breathe.

BUTCH. Yet you can still talk.

SIMON. The bar is calling us back. And we must listen. Everyone with me?

(SIMON charges off. No one follows.)

BOB. Hey, what say we all go back to the bar?

(Everyone ad libs agreement and follows him.)

CHRISTIE. Tommy, what were you doing out here alone with Julie?

TOMMY. Nothing. Jeez, what am I supposed to do – stand outside the bathroom all night waiting for you?

(TOMMY exits.)

CHRISTIE. Tommy!

(TUG remains unmoved. He rubs his knee.)

TODD. What's wrong, Tug?

TUG. I don't know, Todd. I thought it would feel different.

TODD. Your knee?

TUG. The play.

DEBBIE. We should get back inside. It's almost time to give out the awards for people who have accomplished great things.

(to AMY)

Well, you should come anyway.

AMY. That tears it. I need a drink.

FRED "THE HEAD". Psst. I got something better. Step into my office.

(AMY joins him.)

TUG. Wait. Guys. Let's run it again. Come on. Where are you going?

JOHNNY. Let it go, Tug. It was just a catch.

TUG. Not to me, it wasn't! Not to me!

(Most of the crowd walks away.)

JULIE. It was a great catch, Tug.

TUG. Thanks. Sometimes I think I caught it just to hear you cheer.

JULIE. Really?

*(**TUG** starts to go to her. **BARBARA JEAN** interrupts him.)*

BARBARA JEAN. Hey, Tug…

TUG. Hey, Ea-zay…er, Barbara Jean.

BARBARA JEAN. That's okay.

*(**BARBARA JEAN** takes out the photo of her son.)*

BARBARA JEAN. Do you remember the night of the bonfire pep rally?

TUG. Yeah. I remember.

BARBARA JEAN. Tug…I don't know how to tell you this…

TUG. It's not mine, Barbara Jean.

BARBARA JEAN. What?

TUG. I know about your son. People are talking. But…well, I can't have kids. My ex and I wanted them and…well, let's just say I can't be the father.

BARBARA JEAN. Oh. I'm sorry.

*(**BARBARA JEAN** crosses out his name in her book.)*

TUG. Yeah. Me, too. Would've meant at least one of my dreams came true. Sorry. I hope you find him.

BARBARA JEAN. Thank you.

(calling off)

Hey, Johnny? Wait up. Do you remember Senior Skip Day?

JOHNNY. *(off)* Oh, shit.

(She exits.)

TUG.
>DON'T DROP, DON'T DROP, DON'T DROP....
>*(He lets the ball drop.)*
>*(blackout)*

Scene Six

(SETTING: Gym)

(AT RISE: **MISS BLUMQUIST, BOB, MARSHA, MIKE TERZANO, BUTCH, FRED, SIMON** *and* **AMY** *dance.)*

VILLAGE PERSON.

(Song: "BOY SCOUTS USA")

YOUNG BOY
LEARN TO BE A MAN'S MAN
START CAMPFIRES
AND COOK CATFISH IN A PAN
YES, COME, YOUNG BOY
HELP OLD LADIES CROSS THE STREET
GET A BADGE FOR LOOKING NEAT
COME JOIN THE BOY SCOUTS USA

(Every time they sing "Boy Scouts USA" they make a Boy Scout "Be prepared" sign, followed with their arms straight up in the air to make a "U" shape, then an "S" shape, and finally clap their hands to an "A" shape.)

WE ARE THE BOY SCOUTS USA
YOU CAN WEAR SHORTY-SHORTS
WITH A NICE FANCY SCARF
DRINK ROOT BEER UNTIL YOU BARF
COME JOIN THE BOY SCOUTS USA
WE ARE THE BOY SCOUTS USA
SIGN ON THE LINE
FOR A GAY OLD TIME
YOUNG BOY
JOIN THE BOY SCOUTS TODAY

*(***BARBARA JEAN** *and* **JOHNNY** *enter as the dance floor breaks up.* **TODD** *and* **DEBBIE** *enter behind them.)*

TODD. Guys! Hey, guys. Wait. Wait up. While we're all together. I have a little something I need to share with you. It's a long time coming, but I want to get it off my chest. Stay by me, Debbie.

DEBBIE. Gee, Todd, what are you going to say after all this time? Are you really going to do this right here in front of everyone?

(CHRISTIE enters.)

CHRISTIE. Has anyone seen Tommy?

DEBBIE. Quiet, Todd's going to say something! Listen up. You might learn something. Go ahead, Todd.

(TODD takes the microphone.)

TODD. Where do I even begin?

DEBBIE. The beginning's always best.

(Song: "FABULOUS!")

TODD.
> IT ALL BEGAN WITH "CUP CHECK"
> THE TIME BEFORE THE GAMES
> WHEN COACH BELL WOULD BEND US FORWARD
> AND FEEL FOR CUP OR BRAINS

(The guys exchange a look. No one knows what he's talking about.)

TUG. He didn't do that to us.

TODD. He didn't?

BOB/FRED "THE HEAD". No.

CALVIN. No way.

TODD. Hey, come to think of it, I was always alone at Cup Check.

BUTCH. Every time?

DEBBIE. Anyway, Todd…you were saying…?

TODD.
> THEN OFF I WENT TO COLLEGE
> MET MEG AT USC
> GOT MARRIED IN LATE AUGUST
> JOINED HER FATHER'S COMPANY
> BUT EACH NIGHT WHEN WE'D MAKE LOVE…
> I'D BE AN EMPTY SHELL
> WHILE I WAS WITH HER BODY
> MY MEAT WAS WITH COACH BELL

TUG. Jesus Christ.

DEBBIE. I don't get what you're saying, Todd…

TODD.
> I WONDERED WHY I FELT THAT WAY
> BUT KNEW I ALWAYS HAD
> WENT TO A LEATHER BAR
> GOT CHERRY PICKED BY BRAD

DEBBIE/TUG. Oh, shit.

TODD.
> WENT RIGHT BACK HOME AND TOLD THE TRUTH
> CAUSE THAT WAS BEST FOR US
> POOR MEG'S A WRECK
> SHE THREW ME OUT
> BUT ME? I'M FABULOUS!

> *(A driving DISCO BEAT starts.)*

> I'M FABULOUS
> OUT OF THE CLOSET, NOW I'M FABULOUS!
> IF YOU DON'T LIKE IT, KISS MY GAY PATOOTIE
> I'M FRIENDS WITH JUDY
> AND LIFE IS HAPPY AND GAY
> I AM OUT AND PROUD
> HEAR ME – I'LL SING IT LOUD

> I get my back waxed now!

> I AM SO FABULOUS

DEBBIE. But...what about us, Todd? Todd?

ALL.
> HE'S FABULOUS
> OUT OF THE CLOSET, HE IS FABULOUS
> HE THINKS IT'S NEWS BUT, HEY, WE ALWAYS KNEW IT
> WE KNEW HE'D DO IT
> DON'T KNOW WHAT TOOK HIM SO LONG,
> BACK IN SCHOOL
> THOUGHT BARBRA STREISAND RULED

TODD. Well, except for Yentl! Papa, can you spare me?

ALL.
> HE IS/I AM SO FABULOUS

DEBBIE. Where was I?

*(DANCE BREAK, including a chorus line with **TODD** high kicking amidst the football players.)*

TODD.
>DON'T LET ANYONE TELL YOU THE WAY TO BE
>IN THIS COUNTRY WE ALL ARE FREE
>TO BE...
>FABULOUS
>OUT OF THE CLOSET
>I AM FABULOUS!
>IF YOU DON'T LIKE IT, YOU CAN BITE MY BOTTOM
>
>Go ahead!
>
>CUTE CHEEKS? I'VE GOT'EM
>AND LIFE IS HAPPY AND GAY
>FROM FORMER SCHLOMO
>TO HAPPY HOMO
>
>You should see the drapes in my apartment!
>
>I AM SO FABULOUS
>WHO'S GOT THE RIGHT TO TELL ME THEY KNOW BEST
>HAVEN'T THEY NOTICED GOD WORE A DRESS?
>TODD & COMPANY
>I AM FABULOUS/HE IS FABULOUS
>OUT OF THE CLOSET, I AM FABULOUS!/HE'S FABULOUS
>TODD
>IF YOU DON'T LIKE IT, YOU CAN KISS ME GUIDO
>IN MY TIGHT SPEEDO!
>MY LIFE IS HAPPY AND GAY

ALL.
>HE'S SO GAY

TODD & COMPANY.
>I TRADED TEARS FOR LAUGHS/OOH OOH
>I'LL SEE YOU AT THE BATHS/OOH OOH

TODD. I've got the greatest shoes!

TODD & COMPANY.
>I AM/HE IS SO FABULOUS

TODD.
>SO IF YOU NEED ME, JUST CALL
>I'LL BE IN THE NEXT STALL!

DEBBIE. I'm going to be severely ill.

(Dance Break. During the following people use flower arrangements from the tables as hats.)

ALL.

HE'S FABULOUS
OUT OF THE CLOSET, HE IS FABULOUS
HE THINKS IT'S NEWS BUT, HEY, WE ALWAYS KNEW IT
WE KNEW HE'D DO IT
DON'T KNOW WHAT TOOK HIM SO LONG,
BACK IN OUR YOUTH
ALL BUT HIM KNEW THE TRUTH

TODD. I was in denial!

ALL.

SO IF YOU SEE HIM AND HIS MATE
IT'S LEGAL IN FORTY-EIGHT STATES!

*(**TODD** yanks a tablecloth off a table to use as a cape revealing **TOMMY** and **JULIE** in a suggestive clinch. Everything stops.)*

CHRISTIE. Tommy?! Julie!

*(**JULIE** is mortified. Caught and scared.)*

TOMMY. This isn't what it looks like!

*(**CHRISTIE** slaps **TOMMY**.)*

But then again, I didn't see it from where you were.

JULIE. I'm sorry, Christie I –

CHRISTIE. You can both drop dead!

*(**CHRISTIE** runs off in tears. **TOMMY** runs off after her. **JULIE** runs off in the opposite direction, mortified.)*

FRED "THE HEAD". Now it's a party!

BOB. Yet him they voted…

TODD. Shut up. This is my song! Spotlight! Maestro!

ALL.

I…AM…. (HE…IS…) SO FABULOUS…!

TODD. I'm fabulous!

(curtain)

ACT II

Scene One

(SETTING: Ladies Room)

(AT RISE: **CHRISTIE** *is sobbing at the sink. A toilet flushes.* **MIKE TERZANO** *enters from a stall. He washes his hands at the sink.)*

MIKE TERZANO. Are you hurting, beautiful lady?

CHRISTIE. Are you talking to me? What are you doing in here?

MIKE TERZANO. I never use the men's room. Men are generally ill-mannered unmanicured slobs. And…oh, be still my beating heart. I am undone!

(reading name off her tag)

Christie…you are as exquisite as you ever were, a ravishing creature. And once again, the very sight of you heats the cockles of my loins.

CHRISTIE. Yeah? Well, I'm a married woman, so keep your cockle to yourself.

MIKE TERZANO. Oh, don't tell me. You married…oh, what was his name?

CHRISTIE. Tommy Beekman.

MIKE TERZANO. Yes. Tommy Beekman. My arch nemesis.

CHRISTIE. Yes, isn't he awful? Oh, why did we come here? How could he do that? And with Julie Ryan!

MIKE TERZANO. That's the trouble with high school reunions. People become unhinged. They say and do things they'd never do in the light of day. It's a dangerous place for vulnerable women…like you.

(He moves in.)

Especially one so beautiful.

CHRISTIE. How drunk are you?

MIKE TERZANO. The only thing I want to drink is you with mine eyes. What kind of man neglects a woman such as you for a woman such as she? I'll tell you what kind. A fool. A heel. A cad. You deserve better. You deserve the best. You deserve…me.

CHRISTIE. Who ARE you?

(Song: "MIKE TERZANO")

MIKE TERZANO.
THEY SAY I'M THE WORLD'S GREATEST LOVER
THAT ONCE A WOMAN'S WITH ME, THERE IS NO-O-O-O OTHER

There is no other.

(Spanish toreador music.)

MIKE TERZANO
I'M MIKE TERZANO
I'M MIKE TERZANO
I WILL PLAY YOU LIKE YOU ARE A GRAND PIANO
I'M MIKE TERZANO
I'M MIKE TERZANO
BEFORE THE NIGHT IS OVER YOU WILL SING SOPRANO
I'M MIKE TERZANO
I'M MIKE TERZANO…
IN ITALIAN, ATSA MIKE TERZANO
I'M MIKE TERZANO
I'M MIKE TERZANO
THEY ALL KNOW ME BY MY MUSTACHE AND MY TAN-O
I'M MIKE TERZANO
I'M MIKE TERZANO
I MAY USE HAIR SPRAY BUT I'M STILL A MACHO MAN-O
I'M MIKE TERZANO
I'M MIKE TERZANO…
IN MY NATIVE TONGUE, THAT'S MIKE TERZANO
I WILL TEACH YOU THINGS THAT OTHER MEN CANNOT
AND AFTER I TEACH THEM, OH BOY, ARE YOU TAUGHT
YOU WILL CLAMOR FOR MORE OF MY MOORISH AMOR
THE ONE THING I PROMISE IS YOU WILL COME BEFORE

YOU WILL COME BEFORE
MIKE TERZANO
I'M MIKE TERZANO
WE CAN DO IT HERE OR IN THE LADIES CAN-O
I'M MIKE TERZANO
I'M MIKE TERZANO
EITHER LAST ALL NIGHT OR WHAM BAM THANK YOU MA'AM-O

(Your choice!)

I'M MIKE TERZANO
I'M MIKE TERZANO
IN PIG LATIN, IKE-MAY TERZANO

(They dance.)

MIKE TERZANO
COME AND LOSE YOURSELF FOR AN HOUR
I'LL MAKE LOVE TO YOU WITH ALL MY POWER
EVERY INCH OF YOU I'LL DEVOUR
AND AFTERWARDS I'LL LET YOU SHOWER
WITH MI-I-IKE TERZANO

Ole me!

CHRISTIE. Lock the door.

(blackout)

Scene Two

(SETTING: Gym)

(AT RISE: A small group is on the dance floor, rocking out to a record from 1979. **AMY** *dances by herself – like a lunatic.)*

ALL.
>HOW LONG YOU GONNA MAKE ME WAIT
>MAKE ME WAIT
>I'M OUT OF MY MIND
>CHRISTINA

AMY. God, I have so much energy! Look at me!

FRED "THE HEAD". Ah, Jeez. What pocket did I give you that stuff from?

ALL.
>YEAH, YOU KNOW IT'S FATE
>KNOW IT'S FATE
>I GOTTA HAVE YOU TONIGHT
>CHRISTINA

(TOMMY runs in, looks around frantically.)

TOMMY. Fred, have you seen Christie?

FRED "THE HEAD". No, man. I'm not even sure I'm seeing you now.

BOB. Class act under the table, Tommy. Yet you they voted "Most Likely to…"

(TOMMY ignores him and exits the opposite side.)

ALL.
>I'M NOT GIVING UP
>I'M GETTING YOU
>OH, YOU MAKE ME HOT

(BARBARA JEAN approaches FRED on the dance floor, with her little book.)

BARBARA JEAN. Fred, we never uh…you know?

(She gives him a knowing look. It takes him a second to get what she's asking.)

FRED "THE HEAD". How the hell would I know?

(**BARBARA JEAN** *exits, making a note in her book.*)

ALL.
AND YOU KNOW YOU DO
GIVE ME EVERYTHING YOU GOT
NOW NOW NOW OO EE YOW!
NA NA NA NOW
CHRISTINA
NA NA NA NOW
CHRISTINA
NA NA NA NOW
CHRISTINA
NA NA NA NOW
CHRISTINA

(*The music ends.* **AMY** *continues to dance.*)

BOB. I've still got it.

MARSHA. Yes, you do. How about me?

BOB. You have taco sauce on your chin. You might want to go clean that up. Remember, you're representing me.

MARSHA. Fine. Your fly's open. I guess you're representing the little people.

(**MARSHA** *exits.* **BOB** *zips his fly up again.* **JULIE** *looks around frantically. She has a drink in her hand.*)

JULIE. Fred, have you seen Christie?

FRED "THE HEAD". Did you just ask me that?

JULIE. No.

(**JULIE** *exits the opposite side.*)

FRED "THE HEAD". That chick is so into me.

(**SIMON** *approaches* **BARBARA JEAN**. *She smiles and hands him her empty plate.*)

SIMON. I'm not the waiter. But I could be the father.

BARBARA JEAN. What? What did you say?

SIMON. It's me. Simon. Simon Groupie. Remember that night in the backseat of my father's Pinto? You kept calling me "Paul."

BARBARA JEAN. I remember the Pinto.

(**BARBARA JEAN** *walks away.*)

SIMON. Ah, what's the use?

(**SIMON** *sits at* **BUTCH***'s table.*)

BUTCH. Butch Fuorry.

SIMON. I know.

BUTCH. Wow. You know, this is the first time anyone's ever eaten a meal with me in this building.

(trying to place him)

Did you marry someone from my class?

SIMON. No. I'm in this class. We were lab partners for three straight years.

BUTCH. Really?

SIMON. You know, you and I should have been best friends. We have a lot in common.

BUTCH. What? You used to smell, too?

SIMON. No.

BUTCH. *(defensively)* Good. Cause that's MY thing.

(**BUTCH** *moves away.*)

SIMON. *(to himself)* What do I have to do to get noticed around here?

(**SIMON** *walks off, banging into* **MISS BLUMQUIST**.)

MISS BLUMQUIST. Sorry. I didn't see you.

(**CALVIN** *enters.*)

Calvin, are you following me around?

CALVIN. Maybe. Okay. I've got to just say it. Did you ever run into a teacher of yours thirty years later and still think she was the hottest woman to ever walk the face of the earth, Miss Blumquist?

MISS BLUMQUIST. No. No, I can't say I ever did, Calvin.

CALVIN. I stand erected...corrected. I guess I'm still a little tongue-tied around you, Miss Blumquist.

MISS BLUMQUIST. Well, we can't have that.

(Song: "BLUMQUIST'S TURN")

CALVIN, YOU'RE A MAN NOW
THAT'S SOMETHING PLAIN TO SEE
STILL FUNNY, SMART, AND CHARMING
WHICH IS HOW I KNEW YOU'D BE
NO LONGER JUST MY STUDENT
BUT WITH SO MUCH MORE TO LEARN
SO COME PUT OUT THE FIRE

THAT FOR THIRTY YEARS HAS BURNED
COME ON AND BANG MISS BLUMQUIST
COME ON AND BLOW MY MIND
COME ON AND BANG MISS BLUMQUIST
COME ON AND BANG ME BLIND

COME ON AND BANG MISS BLUMQUIST
I'VE BEEN WAITING FOR YOU
COME ON AND BANG MISS BLUMQUIST
COME ON AND BANG ME BLUE

CALVIN/MISS BLUMQUIST.

COME ON AND (I'M GONNA) BANG MISS BLUMQUIST
COME ON AND (I'M GONNA) BLOW MY (YOUR) MIND
COME ON AND (I'M GONNA) BANG MISS BLUMQUIST
COME ON AND (I'M GONNA) BANG ME (YOU) BLIND

COME ON AND (I'M GONNA) BANG MISS BLUMQUIST
I'VE BEEN WAITING FOR YOU
COME ON AND (I'M GONNA) BANG MISS BLUMQUIST
COME ON AND (I'M GONNA) BANG ME (YOU) BLUE

*(**MISS BLUMQUIST** holds her hand out.)*

MISS BLUMQUIST. Gum.

*(**CALVIN** spits it into her hand.)*

Teacher's Lounge. Now.

(They exit together to PLAYOFF.)

JOHNNY. It's always the little guys. Pay up.

*(Money changes hands between **JOHNNY** and **BUTCH**. They exit. **DEBBIE** enters to set out awards on a table. **TODD** follows.)*

TODD. Debbie. Stop. Talk to me. Please.

DEBBIE. I have nothing to say to you, Todd. You're fabulous. I get it.

TODD. I never meant to hurt you.

DEBBIE. You said you spent thirty years looking for what WE had.

TODD. I did. But with a guy. I never knowingly led you on. Even back in high school. What did I do to give you the impression we had a future together? Didn't you find it odd that I never came on to you – even that time you walked around topless in your basement?

DEBBIE. Omigod. All these years I just thought I had an ugly chest!

TODD. I love you, Debbie. Just not that way. You've got to move on.

DEBBIE. To what? I'm almost fifty.

TODD. Just let yourself be open. Maybe someday you'll find what I've found with Hal.

DEBBIE. "Hal?" He sounds all wrong for you. What's he like?

TODD. Well…he's blonde. Glasses. Big blue eyes. About your height. Flat stomach. Firm chest.

*(**DEBBIE** reacts.)*

I'm sorry, Debbie. It was never going to be our story.

DEBBIE. Oh, Todd.

(Song: "I'LL NEVER DANCE WITH YOU")

I'LL NEVER DANCE WITH YOU
I LOVE YOU MORE THAN IT WAS RIGHT TO DO
I'VE WAITED FAR TOO LONG
FOR SOMETHING THAT WAS WRONG
I'LL NEVER DANCE WITH YOU
THE HAPPY ENDING I DREAMED WON'T COME TRUE
IN YOUR ARMS I DON'T BELONG
SO WHEN THE MUSIC PLAYS

THERE'S YOU
THERE'S ME
BUT THERE CAN BE NO "WE"
AND WE WILL NEVER HEAR OUR SONG

(**TODD** *offers his hand.* **DEBBIE** *takes it.* **DEBBIE** *and* **TODD** *dance a la Fred and Ginger.*)

DEBBIE/TODD.
SO WHEN THE MUSIC PLAYS
THERE'S YOU
THERE'S ME
BUT THERE CAN BE NO "WE"
AND WE WILL NEVER HEAR OUR SONG

(*As lights restore,* **JOHNNY**, **BUTCH**, **FRED**, *and* **CHRISTIE** *enter.* **CHRISTIE** *looks around frantically. There is a long piece of toilet paper on her shoe.*)

CHRISTIE. Has anybody seen Tommy?

FRED "THE HEAD". No.

(**CHRISTIE** *exits the opposite side.*)

Hey, is it just me, or did she get really hairy since high school?

JOHNNY. Hey. Isn't that the way Julie and Tommy just went?

FRED "THE HEAD". Yeah.

BUTCH. Then what are we standing here for?

(**DEBBIE**, **TODD**, **JOHNNY**, *and* **BUTCH** *follow. The room is empty. A beat, then* **SIMON GROUPIE** *streaks the room, running figure eights and whooping it up. No one is there to see him. He is nude except for a football which he holds in front of his privates.*)

SIMON. Bet you'll notice me now!!!! Look at me! Look at me...!

(*He raises both arms. The football never moves.*)

Look at me!!

(*He pulls a piece of paper out of his butt and reads it.*)

"I'm a valuable human being!" Aw, never mind.

(*blackout*)

Scene Three

(**SETTING:** *Football field*)
(**AT RISE:** **TOMMY** *runs out onto the football field.* **TUG** *is laying there, tossing a ball to himself up in the air.*)

TOMMY. Tug? Have you seen Christie?

TUG. You blew it, man. And I know from blowing it. You had it all right in your hands and you dropped the ball.

TOMMY. I don't even know what happened. I guess for a minute there with Julie I felt like I was seventeen again. And I had a chance to live my life over. But…I don't want to live my life over. I love my wife. Warts and all. And I mean that, you know, literally.

TUG. Don't tell me. Tell her.

(**TUG** *rises.*)

TOMMY. You're not going to sing again, are you?

(**TUG** *thinks a quick beat.*)

TUG. Nah.

(*He crosses off.* **JULIE** *runs on with the champagne bottle.*)

JULIE. Oh, Tommy. What did we do?

TOMMY. I don't know. I feel so dirty.

JULIE. I thought it would be like it was thirty years ago. But, Jeez, Tommy. Kissing you was like sticking my face in a bowl of soup.

(**TOMMY** *reacts.*)

TOMMY. It's not my fault. I'm used to a much bigger mouth.

JULIE. I came here tonight to feel better about myself and now I feel awful. Poor Christie. I know what it's like to find someone you love in the arms of somebody else!

(**CHRISTIE** *runs on followed by the rest of the classmates.*)

CHRISTIE. Get away from my husband. He's mine. And I'm not giving up without a fight.

TOMMY. It's okay, Christie, I –

CHRISTIE. Shut up, Tommy. This has nothing to do with you.

(**TOMMY** *reacts.*)

JULIE. Christie, it's not what you think.

(*A crowd forms.* **AMY, BARBARA JEAN, MARSHA, MIKE TERZANO,** *and* **TUG** *join them.* **TUG** *is now back in his suit.*)

CHRISTIE. You stuck-up conceited bitch. Just because your husband left you, you think you can have mine?

JULIE. Will you just listen? I don't even want him –

CHRISTIE. You don't even know him. You think Tommy's a funny, cute, rich, successful doctor. But the joke's on you! He's not rich. He's not successful. He's not even a doctor. He's a junior pharmacist at CVS!

(*Everyone reacts.* **TOMMY** *is mortified in front of the others.*)

BOB. What did she say?

CHRISTIE. You don't love him! You're in love with the memory of a seventeen year old boy. Before life kicked him in the teeth. Before he flunked out of medical school, before we filed for Chapter 7, before the IRS took our house and we had to move into a cramped little trailer. Now I work at the car wash and he has a second job at kid's parties making balloon animals.

TOMMY. Stop defending me.

JULIE. He's yours. He always was. So, stop yelling at me because I did the same thing you did thirty years ago.

(*She walks away.*)

TUG. Come here, Julie.

(**TUG** *goes to* **JULIE.**)

BOB. You're broke?

(**TOMMY** *looks up to see everyone looking at him.*)

JOHNNY. It's okay, Tommy. It's not like we all didn't know you were faking it all these years.

TOMMY. You heard us singing? I mean, you all knew?

DEBBIE. We've known for years, Tommy. We thought you'd tell us when you were ready.

(Everyone agrees.)

FRED "THE HEAD". Sort of like Todd.

(TODD reacts.)

BOB. How come I didn't know?

BUTCH. Because you never shut up long enough to hear what anybody else is saying.

BOB. What? That's not true. And another thing –

TOMMY. Stop it! I don't care about that.

(to CHRISTIE)

I don't want to lose you, Christie.

CHRISTIE. Lose ME? You sure you don't want Julie? I mean, look at her. She's hot and I'm not. She's not too shabby and I'm just flabby.

FRED "THE HEAD". Hey, I've got one. She's a "Babe." And you're "Babe Goes to New York."

(off everyone's looks)

What? Oh, did somebody use that one already?

TOMMY. How could you think I would want anyone else? I made the right choice thirty years ago and I wouldn't change a thing.

(Song: "YOU ARE MINE")

YOU MAY NOT BE A BEAUTY QUEEN OR PENTHOUSE PET
YOU CANNOT CLIMB THE STAIRS WITHOUT A LOT OF
  SWEAT
(BUT) IF THERE'S A GREATER BEAUTY – HAVEN'T FOUND
  HER YET
YOU MAY BE CRABBY
YOU MAY BE FLABBY
YOU MAY SWEAR LIKE A SAILOR
BUT YOU ARE MINE

CHRISTIE.
>YOU MAY NOT BE THE SKINNY GUY WHO STOLE MY HEART
>A NIGHT OF SEX WITH YOU IS OVER WHEN WE START
>NUDE PHOTOS OF YOU NOW WOULD JUST BE ABSTRACT ART
>YOUR EYES MAY BE BAGGY
>YOUR ASS MAY BE SAGGY
>YOU MAY HAVE MOLES ON YOUR BACK
>BUT YOU ARE MINE
>IS THAT MY HERO WITH HAIR IN HIS EARS AND NOSE?

TOMMY.
>ARE YOU MY BATHING BEAUTY OR IS IT "THAR SHE BLOWS?"

CHRISTIE.
>YOU MAY ACT RETARDED

TOMMY.
>JESUS CHRIST YOU JUST FARTED

CHRISTIE.
>WHEN I TELL JOKES YOU MAY FINISH ALL MY P –

TOMMY.
>PUNCHLINES

BOTH.
>BUT YOU ARE MINE

TOMMY.
>I MAY NOT HAVE GOOD VISION IN MY CLOUDY EYES

CHRISTIE.
>THAT'S GOOD, YOU MAY NOT NOTICE I'M A LARGER SIZE

TOMMY.
>WHAT IS THAT NOISE? OH, JUST THE RUBBING OF YOUR THIGHS

CHRISTIE.
>YOUR FEET ARE DISGUSTING

TOMMY.
>YOU'RE ALWAYS BALLBUSTING

CHRISTIE.
>YOU GET UP TO PEE FIVE TIMES A NIGHT

BOTH.
>BUT YOU ARE MINE

CHRISTIE.
> I MAY TURN YOUR STOMACH

TOMMY.
> I MAY MAKE YOUR SKIN CRAWL

BOTH.
> BUT, OH, HOW I LOVE YOU

(TOMMY kisses her hand. Reacts.)

TOMMY. Chicken?

BOTH.
> CAUSE YOU ARE MINE
> YES, YOU ARE MINE

(TOMMY twirls CHRISTIE to end the song with her sitting on his lap. Instead, weight of her crushes him and they collapse to the ground.)

BOB. Well, I think it's only fair to say everybody here owes me an apology.

(pointing to himself)

Most Successful! Say it! Say it!!

TODD. What is wrong with you?

DEBBIE. What is your problem?

BUTCH. He can't get over the fact there's something in his life he didn't win.

TOMMY. Well, that. And the fact that he's bald.

BOB. Liar!

(BOB slaps him. TOMMY recovers.)

TOMMY. Did you just slap me?

MARSHA. He didn't mean it.

BOB. I'm sorry, I don't know why I did that.

BUTCH. You have major issues.

TOMMY. I know why. It's been eating you up for thirty years that I got that award. The great and powerful Bob Fields can only –

(BOB punches TOMMY in the face. TOMMY recovers.)

Ow.

BOB. Jesus, I'm sorry.

TOMMY. Oh, so you wanna fight dirty, eh? Okay. That's good to...

(**TOMMY** *punches* **BOB** *in the face as well.*)

BOB. Ow.

TOMMY. ...know.

(**BOB** *raises his fists.* **TOMMY** *does the same.*)

FRED "THE HEAD". Oh, it's on now!

MARSHA. Omigod, Bob, have you lost your mind?

(**BOB** *kicks* **TOMMY** *in the groin.* **TOMMY** *doubles over. Then punches* **BOB** *in the crotch. They roll around on the ground.*)

ALL. Fight! Fight! Fight!

(**TUG** *crosses to* **JULIE** *to protect her from the fight.*)

DEBBIE. I'm telling the teacher!

TODD. Stop it. Stop everybody! Jesus, Mary, and Sweet St. Sondheim!

(**DEBBIE** *and* **TODD** *exit as* **CHRISTIE** *tries to pull* **BOB** *off.*)

MARSHA. Get your hands off him.

CHRISTIE. Fine. I'll put them on you.

(**CHRISTIE** *and* **MARSHA** *get into it.* **AMY** *jumps between them all.*)

AMY. Stop. Stop it. What the hell is wrong with you people?

JOHNNY. Oh, now you did it. You made Mommy mad.

(**DEBBIE** *and* **TODD** *return.*)

AMY. Screw you, has-been. You know, I've had just about enough of you people. "What's Amy been doing all these years?" "Nothing – she's just a mother!" Well, if it weren't for mothers, none of you would be here. And at least I know who the father of my goddamn kids is. I know. You all went and did big things. Well, I raised three kids that are gonna go out and do better things than you. There's my legacy! That's not nothing. That's something. And if you don't like it, you can all kiss my big fat small-town child-rearing ass.

(**AMY** *shakes her small-town ass. There is a beat as everyone reflects. Then:*)

DEBBIE. Get her!

(*Everyone jumps her and the brawl continues, moving offstage in a huge clump.* **TUG** *and* **JULIE** *are left behind.*)

JULIE. Wow, does this happen at all the reunions?

(**JULIE** *drinks from the champagne bottle.*)

TUG. No. Usually nobody shows up and Butch and I just get drunk and watch Fred pee in the potted plants at the Squire's Pub. Are you okay?

JULIE. So I made a fool out of myself. I can handle it. I'm the bitch, remember?

TUG. No, you're not. You're a nice person. You were the first one to call me when I blew out my knee. Don't let them make you into something that you're not.

JULIE. It never changes. All because I was born with good genes and a rich family. I can't help the way I look.

(*starting to cry*)

It's not my fault Christie sat in the sun for thirty years eating pie and potatoes. Let them call me what they want. I don't care anymore.

TUG. Aw, Julie, yes you do. You always have. That's one of the reasons you came tonight.

(**JULIE** *takes another swig of champagne.* **TUG** *takes the bottle away from her.*)

JULIE. Isn't this where I came crying to you after I found Christie with Tommy? I don't know what I would have done if you weren't here that night.

TUG. Oh, Julie, don't you know? I've always been here.

JULIE. Really?

(*hiccups*)

Why?

(Song: "I HAVE WAITED A LIFETIME")

TUG.

> MOMENTS AGO
> WHEN WE WERE STILL YOUNG
> YOU SMILED AT ME AND I WAS UNDONE
> YEARS AND LOVERS ROLLED ON BY
> IT'S ALWAYS BEEN YOU
> TONIGHT I KNOW WHY
> I HAVE WAITED A LIFETIME
> FOR I ALWAYS KNEW
> THAT SOMEDAY, SOMEWAY
> I'D BE WITH YOU

JULIE.

> FOREVER LOST
> AND ALWAYS ALONE
> DEEP IN YOUR EYES
> I CAN SEE MY WAY HOME
> AND THE TEARS AND THE PAIN
> ALL FALL AWAY
> BUT HERE IN YOUR ARMS
> ALL I CAN SAY
> I HAVE WAITED A LIFETIME
> FOR I ALWAYS KNEW
> THAT SOMEDAY, SOMEWAY
> I WOULD FIND YOU

(They slow dance.)

TUG.

> AND THE YEARS AND THE PAIN
> ALL FALL AWAY
> CAUSE SOMEDAY, SOMEWAY
> YOU LOVE ME TOO

(At the end of the song they kiss. The kiss breaks and **JULIE** *projectile vomits all over* **TUG***'s face and chest.)*

(blackout)

Scene Four

(SETTING: Gym)

*(AT RISE: **SIMON**, fully dressed, sits alone at a table. He looks around. He's alone. He crosses to center stage. He rips up his "valuable, worthwhile human being" note and begins to sing.)*

(Song: "SIMON SAYS")

SIMON.
NOBODY SEES ME
IT'S LIKE I'M NOT HERE...!

*(An angry mob enters in the midst of a brutal fight. They sweep past **SIMON** and he disappears inside the crowd, ending his song.)*

BOB. Hey, Tommy. Here's your award. Most Likely to Suck my ass!!

*(**BOB** clocks **TOMMY** with an award.)*

TOMMY. Ow!

*(**TOMMY**'s forehead bleeds.)*

Don't get blood on this suit. I have to return it on Monday!

*(**TOMMY** grabs **BOB** by the throat and they crash through a table.)*

DEBBIE. Stop! Those are rentals! Oh, the deposit!

*(**TOMMY** and **BOB** keep kicking each other in the groin.)*

JOHNNY. Twenty on the fat man!

*(**TOMMY** and **BOB** look up.)*

Bob.

*(**TOMMY** laughs.)*

BOB. Bastard!

*(Finally, all spent, **TOMMY** and **BOB** lie there. **BOB** staggers up. He looks down at **TOMMY**.)*

BOB. *(cont.)* Omigod, Tommy. I'm sorry. I...I don't know what came over me.

TOMMY. That's okay.

(BOB reaches out his hand to help him up. TOMMY punches him in the crotch. BOB goes down, flipping up his toupee to reveal a bright red birthmark.)

BARBARA JEAN. Omigod.

(BARBARA takes out her photo and compares it to BOB's head.)

That birthmark. Preston has the exact birthmark. In the exact same spot. It's an exact match! It's you!

(All action stops as BOB is discovered to be the father. People gasp.)

BOB. What's me? Why are you all looking at me like that?

TODD. Good news. You're a daddy.

FRED "THE HEAD". You her baby daddy.

BOB. What?

BARBARA JEAN. It's true. My son Preston is your son. You're his father.

JOHNNY. Who had Bob? Pay up.

(Money changes hands between JOHNNY, FRED, and BUTCH.)

MARSHA. Bob?

BOB. I never...we didn't...Omigod, we did it in the AV room. Right after that last student council meeting.

MARSHA. Zip it! Have you lost your mind?

(to BARBARA JEAN)

Look, I don't know what scam you're trying to pull here, Eazay BJ. But I have stood by this man for twenty years through countless fund raisers, mind-numbing political speeches, thousands of rubber chicken dinners, millions of sweaty germy handshakes, wearing these boring suits, keeping my hair short and my face frozen in a permanent goddamn smile, to make him

Senator Bob Freaking Fields. So do you really think I'm gonna let some small-time two-bit fortunehunting slut try and blackmail us? I will make this man at least vice-president and I don't care who I step over, push aside, run down, or crush to get him there!

FRED "THE HEAD". I am so turned on right now.

BOB. You have a son? Why didn't anybody tell me?

BUTCH. We did. As usual, you weren't listening.

BOB. Well, Marsha…we can test for it and if I am the father of her –

MARSHA. Shut it, Bob. You will deny this to your death. Because if you don't, I for one won't be sticking around when the only job you can get is an Ambassadorship to Asshole-ville.

BARBARA JEAN. I have no intention of going public with this news. And I'm certainly not interested in your money. If that's what I wanted I wouldn't have waited thirty years to find out who the father was.

MARSHA. Then what do you want?

(a beat)

BARBARA JEAN. A kidney.

BOB. What did she say?

DEBBIE. A kidney.

MIKE TERZANO. Thank God I didn't hit on her.

BARBARA JEAN. My son needs a kidney. That's why I was trying to find his father. Preston needs a kidney, and I'm not a match.

BOB. One of mine?

MARSHA. You mean, you want him to give up a kidney to save the life of an old high school friend's son?

BOB. Yeah…are you crazy? Are you out of your mind?

MARSHA. Bob will be honored to donate his kidney.

BOB. I would be honored to donate my…what?

MARSHA. Think of the headlines. Omigod! We couldn't buy press like this.

BOB. Really? But –

BARBARA JEAN. Oh, God, thank you. Thank you so much.

BOB. You do realize I've only got the two.

BARBARA JEAN. Thank you, Bob. I can't believe this. Thank you. And now that I know the truth, I can see it. He even looks like you.

BOB. He does?

(Song: "IT IS YOU!")

BARBARA JEAN.
(HE'S GOT) YOUR CHEEKS OF RED
YOUR BIG BIG BALD HEAD
AND HE'S GOT YOUR SMILE
HE'S GOT YOUR BULBOUS EYES
YOUR BIG WHITE THIGHS
AND HE'S GOT YOUR SMILE
HE'S GOT YOUR SPARE
THAT BIRTHMARK THERE

BOB.
AND SOON HE'LL HAVE MY KIDNEY
WHICH IS ONLY FAIR

BARBARA JEAN.
AND NOW WE SEE

MARSHA.
IT'S YOU

BOB.
IT'S ME

TODD. *(falsetto)*
BUT NOT ME...!

(Everyone looks at TODD.)

FRED "THE HEAD". This is one messed up reunion.

TODD. Well, I think a lot has been cleared up this evening.

BOB. Hey, Tommy. How many kids do you have?

TOMMY. None. Why?

BOB. Because I have one! I have a son! I win!

(BOB begins thrusting his pelvis at TOMMY.)

BOB. *(cont.)* In your face! In your face! In your face!

MARSHA. Good for you, Bob. You beat him. You won. Stop it. Can we go home now?

BOB. With pleasure. In your face!

(**BOB** *gives it one last thrust.*)

JOHNNY. Hey. Guys. Before we call it a night, I have a little something for everybody. We've been through a lot together, and...

(**JOHNNY** *takes the microphone with his guitar.*)

Debbie, is it okay if I sing one song –

DEBBIE. Oh, for the love of God, go ahead.

(**JULIE** *enters with* **TUG**. *He's in his dress shirt without the jacket and she is wearing his football jersey.*)

BUTCH. Hey, look. The football star ended up with the head cheerleader. Who would have thought?

JULIE. Apparently someone had been thinking about it for a long time.

TUG. You know me. I always score right before the clock runs out.

MIKE TERZANO. It's true. You always did.

(**DEBBIE** *pulls* **MIKE TERZANO** *aside.*)

DEBBIE. Okay. I can't stand it anymore. You're not in our class. You're not even listed in the yearbook. Who are you?

MIKE TERZANO. Mike Terzano. I crash high school reunions. There are always jilted lovers, unhappy divorcees, mojito-soaked wives, it's like shooting fish in a barrel.

DEBBIE. That's sleazy and repulsive.

MIKE TERZANO. I know. But it works for me.

DEBBIE. You're disgusting. The thought of even kissing you makes me want to –

(**MIKE** *kisses her passionately. The kiss breaks. She turns to the others.*)

DEBBIE. Whoa. He's good.

(a beat)

GIRLS. I know.

(a beat)

TODD. And how.

JOHNNY. *(into mic)* This song is for all of you. From my next album – "Another Johnny Walker Sunday." The "Johnny" works on two levels.

BUTCH. You really gotta work on those titles.

JOHNNY. I love you guys. And…I just want you to know that no matter where I go, you're always with me.

(Song: "I'LL BE THERE")

WE ALL STARTED WITH OUR DREAMS
BUT LIFE IS HARDER THAN IT SEEMS
IN A MOMENT YOU'RE ALONE
AND SUCH A LONG, LONG WAY FROM HOME

SO IF YOU'RE LOST AND FEELING DOWN
JUST REMEMBER I CAN BE FOUND

ANYTIME
ANYWHERE
CALL MY NAME
AND I'LL BE THERE

THERE ARE MOMENTS SHARED IN TIME
THEY'LL BE FOREVER YOURS AND MINE
ALL THE LAUGHTER ALL THE TEARS
ALL THE MEMORIES THROUGH THE YEARS

IN THE DARKNESS THERE IS LIGHT
I'LL BE YOUR STAR SHINING BRIGHT

ANYTIME
ANYWHERE
CALL MY NAME
AND I'LL BE THERE

JOHNNY. *(cont.)*
>SO REMEMBER TO HOLD ON
>I'M HERE FOR YOU 'TIL TIME IS GONE
>
>ANYTIME
>ANYWHERE
>CALL MY NAME
>AND I'LL BE THERE
>
>CALL MY NAME
>AND I'LL BE THERE
>
>I'M YOUR FRIEND
>AND I'LL BE THERE

>*(A beat as everyone reflects.)*

JULIE. That was beautiful, Johnny.

BARBARA JEAN. Really beautiful.

JOHNNY. Thanks.

CHRISTIE. Makes you think, doesn't it?

JULIE. Sure does.

>*(JULIE and CHRISTIE tear up.)*

CHRISTIE. I'm sorry I stole Tommy from you in high school, Julie. It's just…well, I loved Tommy since we were in second grade and he shoved grass down my pants.

JULIE. Oh, Christie. I'm sorry I was such a bitch.

CHRISTIE. I was so afraid you'd take him back. I was the bitch.

JULIE. No. I was.

AMY. Ah, you both were!

CHRISTIE. I missed my best friend so much.

JULIE. Me, too. Oh, Christie.

>*(CHRISTIE and JULIE hug.)*

BOB. Call my office Monday, Johnny. I'm going to make a few calls to some people I know in the music business. I'll see what I can do for you.

JOHNNY. Thanks, Bob.

TODD. Gee, Bob. That was nice of you.

BOB. What can I say? Being a father changes a person. It's all about listening.

(**TOMMY** *approaches* **BOB** *with an award from the table.*)

TOMMY. Bob?

(**BOB** *flinches.*)

This is yours. "The Most Successful" Award. It should go to you.

BOB. No, you take it.

TOMMY. No, you take it.

(**BUTCH FUORRY** *grabs it.*)

BUTCH. I'll take it.

TOMMY/BOB. You?

BUTCH. Yes, me. I won a Nobel Prize in Chemistry if any of you popular cool people ever took the time to notice!

(**BUTCH** *takes the award. He raises his arms. Everyone flinches and cover their mouths and/or noses.* **BUTCH** *points at his armpits.*)

Nothing!

(**DEBBIE** *sees* **CHRISTIE** *and* **JULIE** *together.*)

DEBBIE. You guys good?

CHRISTIE. We're good. What about you two?

(**TODD** *and* **DEBBIE** *put their arms around each other.*)

DEBBIE. We're fabulous.

(**CALVIN** *and* **MISS BLUMQUIST** *enter.*)

MISS BLUMQUIST. Not as fabulous as we are. Fourteen times!

CALVIN. Three.

(sotto)

Her mind is gone!

(Song: "I'LL BE THERE")

ALL.

>THERE ARE MOMENTS SHARED IN TIME
>THEY'LL BE FOREVER YOURS AND MINE
>ALL THE LAUGHTER ALL THE TEARS
>ALL THE MEMORIES THROUGH THE YEARS
>
>IN THE DARKNESS THERE IS LIGHT
>I'LL BE YOUR STAR SHINING BRIGHT
>
>ANYTIME
>ANYWHERE
>CALL MY NAME
>AND I'LL BE THERE
>
>CALL MY NAME
>AND I'LL BE THERE
>AND I'LL BE THERE
>
>CALL MY NAME
>AND I'LL BE THERE
>I'M YOUR FRIEND
>
>AND I'LL BE THERE
>I'LL BE THERE

(curtain)

*(During curtain call, **SIMON** gets gypped out of his bow when **BUTCH** cuts in front of him for his own bow and others follow suit. **SIMON** apologetically slinks to the background where he remains through the company bows. After company bows, the cast sings one last number.)*

(Song: "BOOMERS")

ALL.

>WE'RE FABULOUS
>WE'RE BABY BOOMERS
>AND WE'RE FABULOUS
>CHANGING EACH DECADE – AS WE'VE GONE THROUGH IT
>WE'LL ALWAYS DO IT
>AND STICK OUR KIDS WITH THE BILL
>WE KEEP WORKING OUT

SO WE CAN ALWAYS SHOUT
WE ARE SO FABULOUS
DON'T LET ANYONE TELL YOU WE'RE OVER THE HILL

MEN.

THANK GOD FOR THAT LITTLE BLUE PILL

WOMEN.

THANK GOD FOR THAT LITTLE BLUE PILL

GIRLS/BOYS.

THEY ARE/WE ARE

ALL.

FABULOUS
WE'RE BABY BOOMERS AND WE'RE FABULOUS!
FOR US THE FAT LADY – SHE NEVER SANG
WE'LL GO OUT WITH A BANG
WHEN WE REACH A HUNDRED AND TEN
WE WERE THE BEST OF CLASSES
YOU KIDS CAN KISS OUR ASSES
WE ARE SO FABULOUS...!

We're fabulous!

(curtain)

(Post-curtain call, **SIMON** *crawls out from under the curtain, without any music and finally gets his bow. He crawls back under the curtain when done.)*

End of Play

PROP LIST

Class Photos from 1979
Folding Table
Name Badges
Clipboard
Pen
Magic Marker
Long Sheath of Photos
Photo of Barbara Jean's Son
Rubber Chicken
CDs
Guitar with Strap
Campaign Buttons
Paper Towels
Sponge
Lipstick
Small Notebook
1979 Reunion Decorations
Round Tables and Chairs
Centerpieces (double as hats)
Tablecloths
Plates of Food
Drinks
Wireless Microphone
Notecards with Predictions
Water
Piece of Cake
Glass of Champagne
12 Pom-Poms
Chewing Gum
Money
Box of Awards
Piece of Paper with Affirmation
Football
Champagne Bottle
Breakway Table
Bag of Pot
Lighter

COSTUME PLOT

(All same throughout unless noted.)

DEBBIE:
Black and white print summer cocktail dress with pale green sash, black sandals

AMY:
Snugly fitting knit dress with back zipper split open, plain pumps, purse

FRED "THE HEAD":
Jeans, tuxedo print t-shirt over long sleeved white shirt, sandals
Don't Drop the Ball – add football jersey
Post- Don't Drop the Ball – replace suit jacket

CALVIN:
Seersucker blazer, summer slacks, white shirt, tie, belt with Velcro buckle, dirty bucks.
Don't Drop the Ball – lose suit jacket, add football jersey
Post- Don't Drop the Ball – replace suit jacket

BUTCH:
Grey single breasted suit, white shirt, dark tie, black shoes
Don't Drop the Ball – lose suit jacket, add football jersey
Post- Don't Drop the Ball – replace suit jacket

JOHNNY:
Jeans, tropical print shirt, off-white linen jacket with large pockets, summer straw trilby hat
Don't Drop the Ball – loose suit jacket, add football jersey
Post- Don't Drop the Ball – replace suit jacket

SIMON GROUPIE:
Olive summer suit, white shirt, dark tie, black shoes
Into sheer nude body stocking with attached football at groin
Don't Drop the Ball – lose suit jacket, add football jersey with no number
Post- Don't Drop the Ball – replace suit jacket

MIKE TERZANO:
Plaid sport coat, tan slacks, bubble gum pink dress shirt, print tie, brown dress shoes, boutonniere attached with hook and loop tape, dark brown Errol Flynn style mustache.
Don't Drop the Ball – lose suit jacket, add football jersey
Post- Don't Drop the Ball – replace suit jacket

TUG FENDERMACHER:
Grey pinstripe suit, pale aqua dress shirt, teal tie, black dress shoes, duplicate suit jacket rigged with bladder and hose for "vomit" for "I Have Waited"
Don't Drop the Ball – lose suit jacket, add football jersey
Post- Don't Drop the Ball – replace suit jacket

BARBARA JEAN:
Sexy, low-cut cocktail dress, sheer hose, dressy sandals, purse

BOB:
Navy single breasted suit, white shirt, red tie with small pattern, highly polished black shoes, flag lapel pin, toupee
Don't Drop the Ball – lose suit jacket, add football jersey numbered 2
Post- Don't Drop the Ball – replace suit jacket

MARSHA:
Dark simple, but very stylish suit, simple dark pumps, purse

TOMMY:
Black chalk stripe suit, yellow dress shirt, yellow tie, expensive looking shoes, flashy large gold "Rolex" style watch, pinky ring
Don't Drop the Ball – lose suit jacket, add football jersey numbered 1
Post- Don't Drop the Ball – replace suit jacket

CHRISTIE:
Loud print cocktail dress, high heeled sandals, flashy jewelry, oversized fur coat, large purse, tiara

JULIE:
Short dark plum knit cocktail dress, dark sheer hose, Patten leather dressy sandals, purse
Duplicate of Tug's football jersey- same number, smaller size jersey

TODD:
Light tan summer suit, white shirt, pale green tie, brown dress shoes
"We Had Dreams" flashback-white Members Only jacket, knit shirt, mullet hair piece
Don't Drop the Ball – lose suit jacket, add football jersey
Post- Don't Drop the Ball – replace suit jacket
I'm Fabulous – underdressed hot pink t-shirt with "Drama Queen" in rhinestones

MISS BLUMQUIST:
Sexy knit cocktail dress, long flowing silk scarf, dressy high heels, long earrings

** If substituting dance shoes for women, those noted as sandals should be ballroom shoes.

Also by
Billy Van Zandt & Jane Milmore...

Bathroom Humor
Confessions of a Dirty Blonde
Do Not Disturb
Drop Dead!
Having a Wonderful Time, Wish You Were Her!
Infidelities!
Lie, Cheat, and Genuflect
A Little Quickie
Love, Sex, and the I.R.S.
A Night at The Nutcracker
Playing Doctor
The Senator Wore Pantyhose
Silent Laughter
Suitehearts
Till Death Do Us Part
What the Bellhop Saw
What the Rabbi Saw
Wrong Window!
You've Got Hate Mail

Please visit our website **samuelfrench.com** for complete descriptions and licensing information.

www.ingramcontent.com/pod-product-compliance
Lightning Source LLC
Chambersburg PA
CBHW070646300426
44111CB00013B/2296